Reverse Psychology

a guide to your body, soul and mind

Anabelle Crèmme

ISBN 978-93-5610-220-0
© Anabelle Crèmme 2022
Published in India 2022 by Pencil

A brand of
One Point Six Technologies Pvt. Ltd.
123, Building J2, Shram Seva Premises,
Wadala Truck Terminal, Wadala (E)
Mumbai 400037, Maharashtra, INDIA
E connect@thepencilapp.com
W www.thepencilapp.com

DISCLAIMER: *The opinions expressed in this book are those of the authors and do not purport to reflect the views of the Publisher.*

Author biography

The author was born on July 25, 1997. Since she was a little girl, she has liked to practice art. Her first inspiration started from drawing, painting, and music between the ages of five and seven. From there, she started experimenting with new things like theatre, film, sculpture, and more art-related topics. Graduated in Interior Design, Fashion Design, Graphic Design, Fine Arts, and Pedagogy. Master and President of Art and Creativity Studios Academy, regional writer, and singer.

Other books from the author:

Chang and the Blue Moon Call(2020)

Destined: The next Miller generation(2021)

Consecrated: The beginning(2022)

Ana in the world of colours(2022)

Oriental Art Therapy(2023)

CONTENTS

Welcome!

Welcome to your life, reader! You are growing up, and it means being better, smarter and embrace life as an independent being. Do you know the daily thoughts you have when you are imagining how it will be your lifestyle, attitude, job, closet and everything in your future? When you note about others qualities, can be your friends, family, classmates, boys, girls, men, women or famous people, the one you admire and get inspired to be just like them? These thoughts are part of your dream creating a personality and a person that you will be probably in the future after growing up. You need to practice, try and miss finding out what is your body, soul and mind that suits better to you.

This book was made for those to deal with daily and difficult situations, when there are problems, the first thing you will do is open this book, in this first volume I am showing six different subjects, each one body, soul and mind health practising. The book was created for students in college, graduating in Psychology, and as a guide for young people with difficulties to understand their interior and what to do to make things better than before in your outside.

Acknowledgment

Self-esteem

Welcome to your life, reader! You are growing up, and it means being better, smarter and to embrace a new life as an independent being. Do you know the daily thoughts you have when you are imagining how it will be your lifestyle, attitude, job, closet and everything in your future? When do you note other people's qualities? It can be about your friends, family, classmates, boys, girls, men, women or famous people, the one you admire and get inspired to be just like them. These thoughts are part of your dream, creating a personality and a person that you will probably be in the future after growing up. You need to practice, try and miss, meet your body, soul and mind that suits you better.

This book was made for those to deal with daily and difficult situations. When there are problems, the first thing you will do is open this book. In this first volume I am showing six different subjects, each one related to body, soul and mind health practising. The book was created for students in college, graduating in Psychology, and as a guide for young people with difficulties to understand their interior and what to do to make things better outside than before.

Exam: Before you start reading about self-esteem, think about five or ten good things about yourself and write them down below.

1.I
am____

____

2.I
am____

____

3.I
am____

____

4.I
am____

____

5.I
am____

____

6.I
am____

____

7.I
am____

____

8.I
am____

____

9.I am_______________________________________

____

10.I am_______________________________________

____

Warning: Right, if you are reading and have not written anything yet, you are earning a big zero. Go back and give the exam a try. It is quick, I will wait for you to finish.

If you answered it, but could not write ten things about yourself, only five, it is not a problem to deal with. The objective of this exam is simple, it is about asking someone to write five or ten things about himself/herself, good things, and find out what she/he/you are thinking about. If you are one of those who cannot answer, it might be a bad sign, in other words, low self-esteem. Sometimes it can mean you do not know what is happening in your mind or have difficulties seeing the good side of yourself, and also difficult to open yourself to others. You are afraid to be happy and stalk in your world without trying new challenges, surpass obstacles that keep you trapped, and block your mind, leaving you in a different world called The Land of NO.

The land of NO

Ask ten people if you are smart, what are the chances of one of them responding YES? And what are the chances if they say you are beautiful, funny, cool, brave or athletic? 5%? 10%? 25%? If you think the chances are too low, you are not alone. Who feels like there are not enough to do a thing, are the best people to ask about self-esteem. If a person feels this way and gets out stronger, it will give us hope to motivate others to do the same. Your friend, brother, sister, someone can show what to do and not to do with your life and keep your mind opened away from illusions if you want to grow up as a man or woman, motivated, determined, stronger and safer. For example? Well, read about those who have had a hard time and what advice they have for us.

"I had a friend who was bullied a lot at school, and she loved riding her bike to forget what she was going through at home and school. Her family was very aggressive, she always told me that she suffered at the hands of her stepfather whenever her mother went out to work, and it turned out that she had no one else, only me to comfort her.

One day, she was riding a bike with me when we were taken by surprise by the bad boys from school. They challenged her to ride a bike on a bridge that was almost falling apart and that only after completing it, they would become friends. I warned and urged her not to, but she went anyway to prove that she dared to cross the bridge on her bicycle and that she was not a coward as they called her. It turned out that in the end, she went, the bridge started to shake, shake, break into pieces, and she fell. The worst is that this bridge was not just any bridge, and it was like crossing an abyss, from one mountain to the other. All I saw that day was my friend dying for nothing, and the boys who challenged her didn't even get emotional, they just ignored it and left.

The next day, I did not want to go to school any more, and I was thinking about what had happened, but thinking about it was not going to change the fact that my friend had died because of bullying.

My advice is, even if you are bullied, do not let others put you down and do not be friends with these people because they are not worth it, even if they are popular. A true friend will accept you as you are and never dare you to make such nonsense." (Giovana Carneiro)

Giovana Carneiro lost her friend in middle school because of bullying and even after school, it will always have someone jealous, angry, with bad intentions to make you live unhappy, sad, depressed. Do not let others change your heart, affect your judgement and imagine splitting up from your friends. Love in a friendship matters when you do not have a family or somewhere safe to be who you are, happy and free.

"I was born with an internal physical problem right in the abdomen and to take away what was causing me a lot of pain, I had a surgery on my belly. Turns out the doctors stitched me up in a twisted way and the normal turned into the weird. I had a wavy spine, in the sense that you imagine having everything normal from the torso to up, but from the buttocks down, everything is backward, and you need to walk in a crooked way.

It was annoying at first and until I got used to it, I went through a lot of difficulties. Over time, I decided to accept myself for who I am and that I was grateful that the pain in my abdomen was gone for good, even though after the surgery I stayed that way. Today, I have two beautiful daughters that I carried with great effort and I do not regret having undergone the operation because it was for my best." (Roberta Meirelles)

You will feel better after making wise decisions. In this case, Roberta was suffering pain, and it was not because of appearance changes that made her think about surgery. Of course, some surgeries end up in mistakes and cause damage to your body for an entire life, but if you have at least three of your five senses(sight, taste, listening, smelling, touching), you can adapt and live.

"I do not know what I would do without them, at first I was very agitated and motivated, but after I found out the truth, I started to wonder, why did they abandon me? Or maybe she abandoned me? Why am I with people who have not even carried me and have not seen me when I was born, when I am not even their biological child? Who do they think I am? And I was rebellious, aggressive for days. I did not want to know about talking to them because they never told me about it. Until I discovered another reason for me to be there, they never managed to have a son or a daughter, and that made them think about adopting one. Back then, surrogacy did not exist, so the only option was to adopt somebody. Generally, people adopt more babies than children from orphanages. I am really sad about that too, but when I realised how immature I was in judging my adoptive parents for not being of their blood, I was embarrassed by it. I did not

know anything about them completely, but they have taken care of me up to now, and that is why I have to say thank you for who I am today." (Fernando Carcara)

The land of NO is a Codename given to those who have insecurities and low self-esteem as frequent partners in their lives. During the teenage time, young people spend too much time in the "Land of NO" and end up forgetting a small detail, "The land of NO does not exist at all". When a person lives in the land of NO, it means she is being deceived. It is trapped in a world that seems real, but is completely fake. It is a place where we let our minds travel and inhabit. If you stay there for a long time, the land becomes the only place where you feel safe to be yourself but in a negative mood. It exists among many people, especially teenagers. Each person has their version, but the atmosphere is a shame. People see each other, but they can not see as much as they really can. They consider themselves incompetent, weak, lost, helpless, annoying, or inferior in many ways. An example, there are children and teenagers silently committing suicide in secret, closed, or abandoned places, but what they do not see is the love of the family they raised and gave birth to because they wanted a child, or friends supporting everything when your family is against you, or an organization helping you move forward and be who you are, want to be. Even if your parents are arrogant or boring, sometimes they are right, but in other situations, there are also grandparents, uncles, godparents, aunts, cousins, siblings to give all the support and love, not everyone in the family is bad as many see. Think about it:

Will you have some food after spending the last money because you ran away from home?

Do you think the police will help you find a new home? (sometimes it can not happen, they will just send you back home, to your parents.)

How will you protect yourself from the rain, storms and other natural disasters and weather changes?

Will you accept being dirty without having a place to take a shower?

What about the virus? Will you let Death take you because an unknown virus caught you?

Do you want my help or someone trustworthy? (then read the chapter SOUL)

How do people get there?

People who end up in a shameful spiral never really wanted to go there. Extensive research on what people are during the different stages of their lives has some interesting things to tell us. As an example, think about what you were at the age of nine or 10. How did you live? If you were anything like the researchers said, it is a big bet to say you were friendly, liked to learn and try new things, had a great mood, and sometimes felt like you could take on the world. But was there a time in your life that you started to change your actions and mood? When did you start worrying about how do you look or what other people think about you? If you can answer it, then you are just like the people who participated in our reverse psychology research.

The interesting discovery from these researches was that people change quickly and dramatically. The concern is people's minds range from world issues to superficial thoughts (what do other people look like or what do others think?). For most of them, this made them tense because they felt they can not live up to expectations. Suddenly, they looked in the mirror and started to feel insecure. Look around and worry because it can not compete in terms of intelligence, appearance, friends, dating, hobbies, or talent. What happened to them? The answer is, _"they are in the Land of NO."_ The thoughts inside their heads are:

"I am not good enough."

"I am not smart (intelligent) enough."

"I am not tall enough."

"I am not wealthy (rich) enough."

"I am not athletic (strong) enough."

All the sentences have something in common, the word "**<u>NO</u>**". And these thoughts are the small details starting to mess with a person's life, it was good, but suddenly started to suffer and close itself to the world, hiding and entering the "Land of NO", a non-existent place.

A SHORT STORY ABOUT GIRLS

Let us watch the sudden changes in a girl's life. The best way to explain the story of unsafely is going back to 1950. So let us travel in time and study the subject.

Nowadays, in the XXI century, the old photographs of girls who lived centuries back are always almost a joke in reason, because is in black and white, a hard-working mom cooking delicious meals, wearing a pointed brassiere, a neat jumper, and matching high heels set looks hilarious to us these days. And we can not forget the long, old-fashioned dresses that the women from Mansion rich also wore during this time, which also became a joke. That is how things were in the 1950s, women were the mothers of American culture. Men were the worker bees. Men supported the family and that means women were housewives, had lots of kids, cleaned the house, raised the kids, and made sure everything was in order. The white smile you see on so many girls featured in photographs from the 1950s indicated how proud mothers felt for their daughters. It was up to them to keep things in order. That kind of perfect girl left the scene when the 60s arrived.

In the 60s was the hippie generation and the beginning of women's struggle for equal rights across America. From the streets to the jobs, women wanted to have a chance of success. For those women, making sandwiches and keeping the house clean never again. And the washing machines, the concealer, the makeup, the credit or debit card, the hairdryer, the windshield wiper, the purse, the wallet, the hairbrush were also created, all to facilitate the daily routine. They wanted to enter America's job market.

And they wanted to be treated equally when they got there.

Later in the 1970s, women continued on the path to equality. In that decade, a movement called Feminism emerged. This movement focused on achieving equality for women in different areas of their lives, such as entering politics or earning the same amount of money as men to perform the same task. Feminists fought to give women the right to be themselves, make their own choices, and determine their futures. With the feminist movement fighting for women's equality, the 1970s saw girls advance in different fields depending on how they thought women should occupy themselves to achieve equality. So a group of feminists decided to teach women not to consider the fact that they are determined to do some things and not others. For example, not all women should stay at home and be mothers. If a girl does not want to start a family because she is right in the middle of a professional career, she does not have to, even if she gets pregnant. And it is here, in the 1970s, that the abortion debate started to get more interesting. Radical feminists were fully committed to girls' right to do whatever they wanted with their bodies, no matter what. Other women's groups fought for equality, but focused on other issues. These feminist groups disagreed with women from radical groups such as abortion rights, focusing on social and personal issues.

In the 1980s, women started doing activities that used to be done by men, and nowadays, it seems that the role has been distributed, but women are in charge of everything now and some complain that men are not gentlemen in doing their part, which used to be quite different. Women in the 1980s began to occupy positions of power in companies, earning more money than ever before. They chose when and where they wanted to work and what kinds of lives they wanted to have. They could decide between living in their 50s life or living a different life with the new rules of the 70s and 80s.

I was not born at that time, but a friend of mine named Ludmilla Kate was five at the time, and she said that her mother always admired women in the 80s because it was an intense and unique feminist movement. We finally made it to the 1990s, you would think women would be more motivated and confident. Women of the 70s and 80s made serious progress from the days when women did not decide to be mothers and stayed at home. Was not it had been a big win? According to psychologist Mary Piper, the answer simply might be NO. She wrote a book in the 1990s called Reviving Ophelia, which told how the situation for girls did not improve despite all the progress made. Same rights, pay, and a growing sense of independence were all good things. Because of this, girls face cultural pressures that can force them to shift focus. Half of you want to stay true to whom you have always been. The other half tries to be that person among the cultural standards of society. This is the half of the girl that always tries to live up to expectations, which arouses insecurity and a feeling of shame.

When we look around us, it is easy to see that Mary Piper was right. As 21st-century teenagers, we can feel more than confused about all these different societal reactions. It is like women owe it everything while being beautiful, athletic, professional, mom-to-be of the year, amazing chefs, cheerleaders. And it is because of this that there are many groups with unique and specific characteristics in schools, colleges, and even in religions. All this is an example of how people who live in our society are difficult to fit in, due to social inequalities. These pressures intensify this feeling of shame in girls, rarely for boys. Sometimes we can get so confused about what we were supposed to be that we start to think we have failed in every way.

LIVING LIFE WITH FEAR

If you are a teenager, there are chances that you have lived in the "Land of NO". You may not have gone through this yet, but you probably will, at least once in your life. This is the part you can not change, but you can change the way you respond to these feelings of insecurity. You understand this feeling as a part of your true Self. You understand what goes on inside your mind, being something you can control yourself.

DROPPING AWAY FROM YOUR TRUE SELF

Confident and aware of your abilities? This is how it starts when a person feels like using their true self to face the world. The opposite of that is just hiding, depression, worries, and all those bad feelings because you can not measure up to it. When you feel this way, it can lead you to make decisions you do not want to. You can act in a way that is not you, you can dress in styles that are just the same as everyone else's because you are afraid of being rejected, you can eat something you do not like just to please someone, but deep down you are just rejecting yourself. You start agreeing with things you do not believe in, pretending you do not know the answers to questions, or pretending you do not have a good opinion, to avoid people making fun of you, see you as someone cool like them. Anyway, when doubts and worries start to make you act differently than you normally do, you end up moving away from your true self. Since then, the first time you say "yes" or "no", you are moving away from yourself. And this is a very serious subject to talk about.

Some people, however, try to pretend that this is not the case. They think that people who talk and do things their way are just different. They imagine that these people are simply different, that they were born confident or something. But it is not about whether you were born confident or not, it is about something that made you question yourself. Something made you think about things like "I'm not good enough", "Others are better than me", or "I should not try". If you have said things like that to yourself, then now is the time to make some changes, nothing that affects your true self.

Start watching your thoughts like a hawk. Try to count the number of times during the day when you do not feel good about yourself. Write down the thoughts that were on your mind and the situations that made you feel that on the lines below. At the end of the day, check your list and rate which things on the list do not matter, and let the ones that are important to understand more about. You will likely find that only a few of them are interesting to think about and that most are superficial, like feeling fat or not feeling cool enough to win a guy. Appreciate the little things, like appearance, the main topic that sends people into a spiral of insecurity. Do not let yourself get into that spiral. If you are already inside, do a U-turn as fast as you can.

THOUGHTS   **SITUATIONS**

CONTROLLING YOUR MIND

Controlling your thoughts is a powerful technique to prevent bad feelings from being involved. And it starts with controlling what you say, you may have heard the sentence "think before you speak.", "be careful with what you are saying, find evidence first, and then answer it." or "do not think too much, or you will get stuck in the same place."

Has anyone ever told you about it before? It is usually a way of telling us to be more careful and empathic to others. And that is how we are going to use that saying as well. We are going to get in the habit of learning how to be more polite to one person: Ourselves.

The first thing you should know before you speak is that words have the power to create reality. One of the reasons for the existence of the "Land of NO". Once you hear the words; "you are not good enough", you end up believing it. People create a full reality that they are not good enough because a few words have led them to believe it. I will give some examples below:

Is not it?

Ending every sentence with "is not it?" is a way of asking others to agree with you. Most people end their sentences like it, seeking acceptance from others. They want to hear people agree with their ideas because hearing them makes them feel comfortable, confident that they are welcome or admired. Escape from this trap and just say what you have to say. Your own opinion is good enough, even if it is wrong, even if others fight with you, at least you tried.

I hate my ...

I hate plus you equal Land of NO. Why do you waste time focusing on things you do not like about yourself? Why not improve it instead of keep judging something you hate? The question is, where does it take you? Instead, might know that there will always be things about you that are not ideal, but there is no point holding on to those things, it will always be there. If it is not one thing, it is another, because people are always growing and changing their personalities, about what they are or will be. We get tired of some parts of ourselves wanting to change others, or we get tired of making things or eating some foods, hobbies, and swapping for others. So focus on this power of change, even if you do not know how to live with some part of yourself. Do not focus on berating yourself.

I do not know.

Welcome to the first lie of the 21st century. When you say you do not know the answer, it is a way to avoid speaking what is in your mind, you are underestimating yourself. Speaking our minds is a risk, I will not fool you, but is it as risky as trying to live a life as a person who does not have a strong body, mind, and soul together? If you do not know what a banana is, for example, say at least what you are imagining or thinking; I think the banana is pink, with a yellow peel. Asking for help from people who know what a banana is can also help you understand the story about bananas. Just imagine that the banana is the subject you need to know, but you are afraid to answer because you do not know. That is exactly what we are talking about here.

Be careful with what you are saying, find evidence first, and then answer it.

Who has never heard this sentence or one similar? You must have heard it once, right? Many people, especially the proud ones, speak with complete certainty of what they have to say, for example: "I am smarter than you, as proof, I know that strawberries have vitamin D and not vitamins A, B, and C." Really? If you study nutrition or vitamins in science school classes, you will see that is a complete lie. Strawberries do not have vitamin D, but they are rich in all other types of vitamins. So, the person who answered "correctly" did not research and answered without being careful, to tell the truth. And the truth is "He/ She does not know."

What I mean is, there are a lot of people, when they are stressed, talk about things that have nothing to do with the argument or the situation they're in or when they're opening up to strangers or acquaintances and end up talking so much about themselves that they don't realise what they said about their relationships or wrong attitudes that they had done for ages or weeks ago. The sentence is telling you not only to care when you speak, but also to pay attention to your feelings, your doubts.

Do not think too much, or you will be stuck in the same place.

Some people think so much about a simple question that they get stuck and only realise it later. Imagine that a friend of yours asks you about what you are going to do on the weekend, you start to think about a lot of things before you say what you are going to do. Ready! You are already entering the world of illusion, where it sounds real, but is totally out of the flow. In a simple question like this, if you do not have a direct answer yet, you only need to answer that you are not sure of what you are going to do, but probably will go to the cinema, or will be sleeping on a couch at home, or go out to the club. If you think it is hard to answer a simple question, try talking like in the topic; I do not know.

ONE EXIT

Knowing which words create the feeling of insecurity in you is the first step, and we just realised that. Now, let's turn the power of words to our advantage. Here are some ways to reverse the process:

Recognize cultural pressures

Ask yourself what your culture asks you to do. For example, when you read fashion magazines and books, do you feel like you are being asked to look like the commercial models you see? If yes, make sure what you are doing, what is being asked for. Do you ask yourself to get to know yourself? Or is it a way of expressing what you feel for the culture? Guide yourself by your heart and not the surrounding culture, ask yourself if this is what you want or if it is your mind telling you to follow a different path than your heart asks.

Recognize the differences between the genres

Boys and girls are not the same, no matter what anyone tells them. Although women from the 1950s to the present day have strived to make a world equal for boys and girls, that is not what it is all about. God made us different, and we were born to carry out a mission, a role in this world, that is, to be part of it using our gifts and talents that were born with us. With girls, it happens as follows:

Girls become teenagers, teenagers become women and that is when they realise how hard it is to get a job and work in a place you like, and you do not end up making as much money as a man who does the same job as hers. Others notice this during school when a teacher treats boys as if they are the smartest and girls as if they are the prettiest and most polite. All this is a stereotype that people create girls, multiple incidents in common, or when they do not want to assume the truth and make it up, they create a stereotype about a group of people who have flaws or not-so-perfect qualities.

To avoid becoming this kind of person, use words that do not link genres to success, such as achievements are best for a girl. Focus on yourself and what you can do as a person and not another genre. It is okay if you want or feel is part of LGBTQIA+ community, but try listening to yourself, by feeling and not by reason.

Vanquish the monster could-should-would have

I know that many times when we make mistakes by our actions, we start to say the words in the past tense, we think of countless ways to win back, but we know that we do not have the power to travel in time to fix something from the past or seek to know what will happen in the future. You can not do it all over again, so why use words that emphasise what you could, should, or would have done if you could do it again when you can enjoy your present? Moving forward means making past things better or different. It does not mean you should erase what you did wrong, but fix it in a way that does not have to repeat itself. Use words that allow you to see your future, stop locking you into the past. And then you ask yourself: "How am I going to do this?". The answer to your question is simple, like when you fight with your parents or your friends, try to look for mistakes made by you and not theirs, apologise even if you know how wrong the other person is too. To be honest and clear, I will give two examples below:

"Luís is a famous teenager like those TV pop stars, but he also has a band, and it was in this band that he started to gain his character. One day, he wanted to prove to his friends that he was the person who was in line for fame and not his friends, so they got into a fight, each going to a different country. Until the day of his show, Luís was alone and realised that without his band, Luís was only himself without his character."

And then? What do you think he should do? Hard question? So let us answer what Luís could do to get the band back together and win the trust of his friends back. He could call his friends or leave messages saying how much he made a mistake without seeing the goal and teamwork that makes him stronger and more confident. He might also admit the focus is not just on him, but on everyone in the band. As soon as he does his part, the band may play together again, or it may not, but Luís has already done his part to fix what he did wrong. Remember: "The bond of friendship is stronger than you think."

Now let's look at a second situation, where there is a fight between parents and children.

"Luana is eighteen years old and lives with her parents. She is a girl who likes heavy music like Rock and electronic and K-Pop like the songs played today in the 21st century. Luana always wanted to have a home of her own to play whatever she wanted anytime, which made her become independent, maybe even too independent. One day Luana was leaving college when she saw a house with a sign that says "For sale" and costs 80.00 (Of course, it is just make-believe, a house would not sell for just eighty dollars, right? But let us assume there is). Luana is surprised by what she sees and decides to buy the house, she makes the deal with the real estate company and moves into the new house, and guess what. She had nothing to heat food, store clothes, not even a bed to lie on, and with each day that the water and electricity bills went up, the poorer she became."

Based on these conditions, the only way Luana could do would be to ask her parents for help, and apologies for having run away from home and gone to live alone without knowing the consequences. After all, buying a house to live alone is easy, but living without furniture is very difficult, money works for you and not you for it.

And this was another example for you, reader, to be aware of what you are going to do before it is too late, think twice before going to another one, do not leave exam questions blank, try to answer the questions you have more knowledge of and then answer the most difficult ones, if you do not know anything, at least try to answer them even if it is just to fill in the blanks. But beware of words could, should, and would have done it.

"I could have answered question number eight, but I did not."

"I should have tidied up my room before I left."

"I would have answered correctly if it had not been for the noise outside."

Speak loud and clear

Talk to yourself, talk to other people about yourself. Talking about your strengths or receiving compliments can create a reality where you feel successful. This feeling leads to the individual's confidence, the desire to continue learning, growing, and thriving. It is not talking about your flaws, your personal life, your intimate side, but opening up to your friends, your boyfriend/, and your own family.

Do not you believe you can focus on yourself without feeling like a person who thinks is smarter than everyone else? If you do not understand the question, look up the word "presumptuous" in the dictionary and to understand better read "Philippians 4:8", a bible verse that encourages us to keep our concentration on things that are admirable and excellent. Although it is a bad idea and self-centred, it is always good to look for admirable and splendid things that are inside you, especially your qualities.

Do not take "NO" for an answer

Do not let words create a space in your life that you are not so good at. When you hear bad words in conversation, do not keep hearing them, walk away immediately. But if you start having negative thoughts, calm down and think about what you are saying mentally or verbally as well. Use words that are real. Say things that you know to be true and confirmed by studies and research. Live from your true Self, do not stray from it.

ROMANCE

Well, you must have seen those cheesy advertisements for sure. You know those black and white movies with a guy and a girl who are totally in love with each other, walking through the woods while the river is making slow sounds of the flow, the gentle breeze that blows through the strands of hair and over their faces, and they stare at each other with eyes that burn with passion, and say in a very shabby voice: "I love Calvin Klein perfume."

Yes, the ads are unbelievable. And you ask: "Who put the special effects of the water and the scenery while they are wearing those long clothes?" Even though the ads can be unbelievable, they also send many serious messages. The ads are full of all kinds of references to what we consider to be romantic, just to sell a product. As if the ad images remind us of the things we love to do, read, have fun with friends, or family. They bring the idea and make us feel that we want to wear or use what is being sold, and according to our phrase, the Calvin Klein perfume (this goes for any other object or brand of the product being sold). The central point is to hit people right in their hearts. All this makes us feel the romance, and sometimes it gives that feeling of going out with someone, dating, kissing a person, at other times the feeling of passion and wanting to do something more than just romance.

Nowadays, you do not see much of the attitudes of a man doing everything for women. Attitudes that were considered romantic like a boy opening the car door, pulling a chair from the table, or simply saving a lady in distress may seem strange and unromantic, at most we can say that the boy is polite and kind. These days, guys who do things like that run the risk of being called fools, idiots, or misogynists, because they will not back down and let the girls do things for themselves too. If you are a boy, you know it, and you understand why.

What can you do?

It is not a lie to admit that many children still go home and dream of their charming prince or princess. Wishing a guy would take a girl's foot off the ground might be old-fashioned for modern girls, but that dream is something that still exists. And when it is girls who try to seduce guys to get their attention, it's much more complicated to know if they like brunettes, blondes, light-eyed or dark, tall or short, thin or fat. Everyone chooses their type, but I can be sure you will choose love by heart, and your intuition will tell you who is the right person. This advice is also for LGBTQIA+ people.

Before you start dating, you should think about the possibilities of what you want to work out, if he or she is the right person, whether you can be more than friends or want to be engaged, oops. That is too much, right? Okay, so let us start with romance.

TEN SIGNS THAT YOU ARE AN EMOTIONAL PERSON FOR ROMANCE

- You call radio stations so often to dedicate songs to your love

- You spend your free time baking letter-shaped cakes to form your love's name.

- Your cellphone data is used with text messages that are sent to your love.

- You sing love songs in your mind and include yours and the name of the one you love in the lyrics.

- You have written a love note in lipstick on a crush's car. Or you left a note in the crush's locker.

- Now you are fluent in four languages, love sports, study art, and play video games, all because of the person you care about doing these things.

- You sent flowers, candy, or gifts to win your love's heart.

- When you and your date go out for pizza, you ask the pizza maker to put the pepperoni in the shape of a big heart.

- You pay extra monthly fees to switch photos from his/her camera to yours.

- You practice signing your first name with his/her last name.

EMOTIONAL

So what does all this mean? For emotional people, the diagnosis is: You are quick to fall in love. You probably put a lot of energy into trying to get them to notice you, and you almost always expect his/her action more than yours. You want him/her to fall in love with you in return.

The good on it: Emotions

Being in touch with the sensitive side of our minds is a blessing. In the 21st century world, emotion is often replaced by intelligence. Our world is full of logic and science. And the world simply disregards everything that cannot be proved by facts and figures.

Mind in touch with emotion is a welcome change. Sometimes letting our feelings guide us creates a new perspective on the world. A feeling like the flash we feel when we are excited when we are in love when we are singing and dancing with all our energy and soul, or simply interested in a boy, can penetrate the emotions that people usually keep locked inside. Same. When you're afraid to let your true feelings out, you can miss out on some of life's best experiences. An example is a film called "13 Going on 30", which tells the story of a girl played by Christa B. Allen, where the main character tries to be like the popular girls, but when her wish comes true, she ends up losing her profile and a friend too, if you watch it you will understand better.

The risks in it: Passion and desire

If you fall in love with everyone you care about, your life becomes a teen soap opera. The soap-opera and drama-series relationships that play on television are there for a reason: they do not work in real life. When people get close to each other, it is not like they can just change course in the next episode by falling in love with someone else.

Being an emotional person, you run that risk. Passion is short-lived and usually gets you nowhere. It ends, and you wonder where all that energy went. The second risk is desire when the passion goes too far and the body commands your mind to go down that path. This can lead you to make horrible decisions. Going much further physically as many young Americans do or beginning to understand the emotional, religious values you value may be the result of your desire.

What God says about it: Emotions are gifts

Beware of your emotions, they bring out the best in you. The Bible is full of passages where you are encouraged to use your thoughts, positive emotions, and imagination in the Lord's service.

The best example? The Psalms. Take a book, add a few hundred chapters, put on some old musical instruments, and you willl have song after song filled with emotion. The Psalms are a cry to God, lovers, blessings, friends, nature, animals, music, good health, harmony, good times, and more. Words are not intellectual thoughts. The Psalms speak of emotions and not just words.

Imagine King David in his spare time bouncing around the palace lawns singing feelings from his heart. Emotions, however, also have their cons. Where is the best place to see the risks caused by emotion? Keep reading about the story of King David. His instant infatuation with Bathsheba led to a total mess in his life. Not only did he have sex with someone else's wife, but he also murdered her husband to try to cover the whole thing up.

You must have heard this story a hundred times, but the Psalm is worth remembering if you have not read the Bible because you are not a Christian or because you think Christians only talk about Bible stories, do not make mistakes. Have you heard about the difference between text and context? If so, you know what I am referring to, but if not, I will be straight with you.

Text: It is what is written on paper, but it does not need to be explained in an interpreted way, because anyone can read a text, even without understanding. For example, this book is about reverse psychology, but its context is toward topics within psychology in general.

Context: It is the total interpretation you have of a text. The text may be written with a lot of slang or like a children's story, but all that text has a reason to be written there, they will teach you the meaning and morals of something that you may carry with you all your life.

Emotion turned into passion often ends badly. As I said, the fire you feel at the beginning can eventually burn you down, and you are the one who bears the consequences, carrying guilt, pity, shame, confusion, and a feeling as if you and God are distant or as if you were in a fight.

TEN SIGNS THAT YOU ARE A RATIONAL PERSON FOR ROMANCE

- You like to share the bill when you go on a date.

- You have never jumped in a car with a friend and secretly followed someone you liked just to find out where he/she lives.

- When you go to the beach, you wear a functional swimsuit and not something that "eats you with your eyes". The expression eat with your eyes means something that attracts attention.

- You have never pretended you were not home when a boy called just to make you anxious or to make him/her want you more.

- First, you seek friendship and then romance.

- You know exactly what you are looking for in a boy/girl, and you will not settle for less.

- You do not have dolls or stuffed animals named after your love.

- You feel good in front of him/her even with hair that has not been washed for two days, no makeup (in the case of girls), and clothes that do not match.

- You say: "I want more!"_ when both go out to eat and are hungry.

- You do not care if he or she knows your mannequin size, shoes, and how much you weigh.

RATIONAL

Who are rational, the situation is a little different. For the rational, everything must be equal and divided. You do not start a romance because you have just met after twenty minutes of talking, and you are looking for a sign that your feelings are mutual. But there is the negative diagnosis: All this equality means a lot of waiting to see what will happen in the future onwards. And as time goes on, you run the risk of knowing so much about that person that it makes him/her seem cool, and sometimes you forget that he/she lacks some of the key qualities you are looking for, like being a Christian, for example. It is very rare to find Christians who are not Evangelicals or Jews.

So imagine that you want to talk to a person of the Jewish religion, but you do not even know that he/she follows Judaism until when you get to know him/her even more you discover that he/she is not your type, but still, you fell in love. Then comes a question: Is it a sin to love someone of another religion? And I say that in some cases it can be considered a sin, but that does not mean you can not be together.

I know a girl who is an occultist. Occultists are those who practice witchcraft, but that does not mean she is evil, but on this subject related to religion, we will talk in chapter three. Returning to our subject now, the girl I mentioned lives here in Brazil in Brasília, despite her family being Christian, she follows the occult, and it is difficult for her to fit in with people because she is afraid that they will call her an evil witch, but pay attention, occultism is one thing and Satanism is another. Anyway, she met a boy who follows the Christian religion, she fell in love with him, but does not know what to do, so what would you do if you were in her shoes? Difficult, is not it? And that is why we are going to talk about equality and reciprocity.

What God talks about equality and reciprocity

You might not use that word very often, but if you're rational when it comes to romance, you know this well. Reciprocity is an exchange. You know, I give a little, and you give a little too. When people are rational, they look for exchange. They do not want to be the only ones in love. And they do not want to give up other fun things in their life just to date someone else. This is called preserving the heart. That is to say, protect yourself, since the chances of you are not getting married are very high.

Both are not the same as withholding love unless you get something in return. It is about equality, the feelings are there, but you do not go on a person you just met, change all your hobbies and give up other things you like to do in life.

However, being a rational person can be difficult. When we start to think that we should like someone this way, many of us find it difficult. So, we wait for what will happen to us, for example, if two people who love each other enter the realm of friendship it can be more than many candidates can handle. This is where the rational person hits the spot. He/she stops, looks, and thinks about what is happening before giving his/her heart.

THE RISKS THAT A RATIONAL PERSON FINDS DURING THE ROMANCE

Missionary Encounter: This happens when a person has the "responsibility" to bring their love to Christ, for example, this happens a lot with the girls. That means dating, a serious relationship, and deeper levels of intimacy, all in the hope that in the future, someday, maybe even today, the boy will be converted and come back to God. Even a rational person can not make a missionary meeting work simply because that is his/her plan: God is the only one who can be called Christ, and kissing on the mouth can not do that. Missionary meetings do not always end the way we imagined, and people do not always convert. Hanging out with a guy or a girl can bring growth to our lives. But do not forget that spiritual growth means you, that is, your state yourself. And God is on the same side as you. So far we have seen what a missionary encounter is. Now I am going to talk about marriage. Well, marriage. Imagine you are waiting for your bride at the altar, or you are dressed in your long dress heading towards the groom. But the matter is serious, many young people nowadays prefer to break the rules, first they start dating, after three years they already think about getting married, and then they start to form a family. It is all so fast that the person does not even realise if he/she made a mistake or if they did the right thing. There are no laws that prohibit a person from doing such things, but there are laws saying that to live alone and have a responsibility in the country, you must be a certain age, for almost everything, ethically speaking, it is for everything.

Imagine you, a 16-year-old, suddenly start dating a 17-year-old, you stay together for three years and think that you will fall in love for eternity, but deep down the person does not know much about you. And even you do not know everything about the person. Even so, you legally marry and live together in a shack, raise children and say that life is as it should be. Will it be? And the University? And the school? And your career? This is what we call a sudden marriage. The biggest myth of all this is that everyone says it is okay to date guys or girls who do not follow the Christian religion, since none of us will marry that person. But the reality is that it is very difficult to have a relationship between couples with different religions that are not linked to the Christian religion. Me, for example, I do not have any religion, I just believe in a greater force, my family is Christian, my other family is Spiritist. There is a big difference getting in the way of being who I am, but I am who I am, no one can force me to be what I do not want to be unless I want to change it. Do you understand what I mean by incompatibility? Even if you are not going to marry the person, there are still a lot of things that will be on opposite sides. But in some cases, such as the soap opera Caminho das Índias on Brazilian television, Maya could not marry her true love because he was already promised to another one of her same religion, only that her love was from another religion and another family, so enter our context. It is unlikely that Maya will be able to marry a person of another religion, let us assume that Maya is Christian and the other is Jewish, both can follow the relationship, but follow each other's religion, it may be that one of them converts to the other's religion, but that would hardly happen. However, both accepted each other's differences, both accepted to fall in love and both continued to meet, then we can say that they are made for each other. But be careful, do not start playing house, that is, do not start thinking that the relationship is a doll play, it is not just about kissing, marriage, children, and freedom. And then you ask me: _Romance, but what kind?_

Romance, but what kind?

It does not matter if you are rational or emotional, in the future, you will declare to someone. No, we are not talking about marriage, we are talking about your feelings for someone. To link to romance, you need to follow some advice like following a recipe. Quoting again about that film that we talked about our emotional side, Gabriela said the following sentence:

"I had watched the film "13 Going on 30", but I found it so dull, despite the message that the film conveyed was about the girl finding herself who she is. At first, she is Maria and goes with the others, but when she realises at the age of thirty that she has made a big mess, she regrets it and goes back in time to fix what she had done wrong.

In the end, she has lived the real happily ever after and the film ends."

Indeed, our colleague watched the film, and it is an example of today's girls who are looking to find out who they are pre-teens. We often envy girls who are superior to us, who get boys' attention and ask them to be quiet, but we can not just copy a person's every action. And one thing you should learn is: No matter how hard you try to change yourself, there will always be someone criticising you for your beauty and your features.

Some people start dating

Dating is simple. First, it starts with the true friendship between two people, then both fall in love and start a romance without illusions or disappointments. Because dating means finding a partner to move forward with you through a period of your life. In dating, different actions become the focus of the relationship, quite different from what happens in staying. After discovering the intimacy of the person you are with, you start planning the wedding, two reasons why it started well: friendship and personal knowledge.

Some people start by meeting

These people are called "frivolous", that is, they are people who seek interest in someone, and only for that person, but they do not seek to have a definitive relationship, and it will not be a long-term relationship either. For example, imagine that you are poor and have practically nothing, but you run into someone elegant and tidy, popular and intelligent. At first, you might think it is a rich lawyer, but if you marry him/her, I will not have any problems. Or the boy who bumps into a popular, charming and beautiful girl, then he thinks: This girl is beautiful, I think I am going to start dating her, she must have a lot of money!_ Well, you are not alone, the world is full of fake, selfish, bad people, but the world also has its established orders. Being interested in a person just for specific traits that you find most interesting is different from meeting them and finding out the truth. We think a lot about people just for their appearance, but we never really accept or see the inner beauty, we will talk about that later.

Some people flirt and start dating random people

These people are the most indecisive, they do not even know who to stay with, to marry, or to start a relationship with. She simply walks up to any pretty people or dresses up in exaggerated clothes and makeup to attract attention. The same for boys combing their hair, wearing wonderful clothes, and spraying perfume to attract attention. Who has not looked in the mirror and told themselves, they look beautiful? Of course, everyone has done this, and that is exactly it, people think they are too beautiful on the outside, but they do not find themselves on the inside, because they are not working on it. And where does that take me? If you do not find the right person to start a relationship with, or you do not find yourself within yourself, it means you are not ready, you are not ready yet to endure a relationship or overcome obstacles that will come by the way. But do not think we are going to talk bad things about flirting here. Flirting is completely natural. It is part of the test of what is going on with sexuality and development. Just know that you can not let flirting get out of hand. It is not about getting attention. And you/he/she can even take things that are hard to deal with, like pressure to have sex. Because you use your body to get attention when flirting, it is hard for guys not to get signals that you are interested in them in a physical way. Or because you keep inventing poetry or a romantic performance to introduce yourself to someone without letting it go.

An important advice

Attempting romance is not the same as getting lost in a whirlpool of emotions and excitement. And this is where the advice comes in: keep your head straight. Know what kind of romantic person you are (rational or emotional) and take it easy. The biggest mistake girls make during adolescence is becoming passionate about romance. Girls spend days, hours, and weeks worrying about dating, crushes, and what to do with feelings. Girls can get goosebumps when the guy they like approaches them, or spend their free time dressing up to try to get the guy's attention. Guys, on the other hand, do not worry that much, but every time he looks at a girl/boy and likes her/him, will always follow or admire her/him. So, take your time, take it easy when it is time to fall in love or start a romance. If you are aware that you are not yet ready for the challenge, take a break from romance and start thinking about coexistence between people. Also, your wedding will not be next week.

PREJUDICE AND PERCEPTION

Okay, go ahead and try to complete the sentences with words that fit in the blanks. To understand the issue of prejudice, you need to know what it is, so go ahead and be honest, complete with the sentences that come to your mind, but do not get away from the subject.

Afro-descendants are good at ___________________________.

___________________________ *do not know how to drive.*

Who was born in ______________ *run convenience stores.*

Boys who do ballet are _________________________.

______________ *always get A's and are the best in school.*

Tall people play ___________________________.

When you see people coming your way, how can you tell if they are sexist or not? And as for idiots, punks, Muslims, or homosexuals, how do you classify them? If you could not answer the questions, then you are just like everyone else. So keep doing it. Sometimes you determine a few things about a person right off the bat and then immediately label them. She is boastful. He is a Jew. They are white rubbish. Welcome to the world of prejudice.

The reason I made you reflect on what you think about something or someone is that this is the easiest way to make you realise what prejudice is all about. It is a summary to describe groups of people who act only for appearances and interests. Prejudice is a matter of opinion. It is not based on facts, and it ignores our individuality. Prejudice is an opinion you have without verifying the true information. This is a problem of our society. And as the globe becomes a smaller place due to the information we receive through websites, television, and magazines, society also becomes unbalanced. The United States is one of the most diverse nations on the planet. So they may be richer or poorer, they may have different skin and different dressing style, they may have different religions or cultures, but in the end, we should all look the same. For now, it is considered as the first world power in everything, but soon that could change with the current government of the 21st century.

ONLY ONE LABEL

Some people have pretty faces; others are smart. The whole idea of equality in terms of our physical bodies or our personal qualities and abilities is simply not true. We are not all the same. But we are all the same as human beings. We are all born of a father and a mother, we all have organs to live, think, breathe, we all get nervous, cry, laugh, dream, get angry, envy, and want to live with other people. All of this is part of human nature. That is how God made us. That is what being equal means. It means that under all appearances and abilities, people have the same values. They have bodies, hearts, minds, and souls, just like we do. They were made by God. This is the first point to begin to understand the difference between prejudice and perception.

When prejudice settles in our minds, we forget about it. Instead of seeing people as human beings, we see them as a label. Some are labels of race, others are about how much money people make or where they came from. Either way, the label does not describe people on the inside. It is just a name we use to describe people without knowing exactly what they are. How does this occur? Why are people prejudiced?

IN THE OLD DAYS...

Prejudice is lost in the history of humanity. Do you remember the bible story about the good Samaritan and the New Testament? It is found in the book of Luke. The story tells of the trip of three passengers, where they passed close to a man who had just been robbed by thieves and bandits of that time, and in the end, only one

of them stopped to help the man. The three passengers were a Jew, a Levite, and a Samaritan, all had the chance to help the man, but only the Samaritan stopped to help. The prejudice that is found in the story is that the man who helped the man is usually the most rejected in history.

In ancient times, Samaritans were the lowest social caste. So when Jesus told us this story, people would probably have thought that the Jew or Levite would stop and help the man, not a Samaritan. Every generation that has passed has had to deal with people who looked down on, were violent, rude, or aggressive in opposition to some other group. History shows us the Caucasians who oppressed American slaves; Nazi Germans who hated the Jews, the American fear of the Japanese, and, recently, Muslims who try to destroy Americans (9/11).

But we've also seen other examples. In America, Native Americans were often murdered and beaten for practising witchcraft. African Americans used to be segregated, inferior citizens because of skin tone. Women did not have the right to vote. In the two examples that were cited above from the story of the Samaritan to the 9/11 attack, we can understand that it is all about stereotypes, misinformation, and fear.

STEREOTYPES

The facts of the stereotypes, that tend to remain, are generally true. For example, many people who are tall and enjoy sports play basketball. Think about it, the basket is already high, few short people will make it to the team, why? Because the basket is high, and the person is tall, there are many chances that he will make the basket, but if the person is short and the basket is high, there is little chance that he will make the basket and thus be able to join the team. Thus, a stereotype can be considered true, in part. But this is where stereotypes lead to prejudice: when you only see the stereotype and not the person. For example, a girl with a short stature tries out for the basketball team. She ends up being cut. But instead of people telling her she did not do well on the test and the coach cut her in two minutes, people say, *"Short people like you will always get cut in basketball."* What? *"They are dwarfs!"* In general, people can not use stereotypes without being prejudiced. In the example given above, a short person could not play basketball. This makes the stereotyped individual feel diminished and begin to change their attitude. So when you hear something about her without knowing the person, you end up believing the stereotype and not the right quality of the person. There are three things you end up extracting from this story:

Stereotypes can never describe an entire group of people. Everyone is an individual. No words can describe this kind of diversity.

Stereotypes are usually only half the problem. The other half of the issue is prejudice. If you believe the stereotype, the next step may be hated.

A mindset that is based on stereotypes and prejudices will be unable to follow Jesus' commandments, which tells us to love one another. And even in other religions, they say that we should respect our neighbour.

MISINFORMATION

Too often, misinformation comes to us in two categories: rumour and media. To better understand what it means, see the meanings below.

Rumours

What is it?

Do you know what happens when a friend or a person tells someone else something they heard through someone else? Yes. Rumours. And the true thing about a rumour is that much of it is untrue. The same goes for disinformation when it comes to prejudice.

The prejudiced rumour can take many forms. He can gossip about silly things like what a person eats or what they look like. Or it could be a rumour that they matter to a person, religion, or family.

Prejudiced rumour is equal to mean talk. And so rumours start to spread about it.

What to do?

If the rumours are about you, the first thing to do is report them, even without knowing who spread the rumours. Even if it is not with you, and it is with someone else or a friend of yours, help him or her.

SPEAKWhen you hear people spreading rumours, Stop and change the subject immediately, or call your friends for a private chat.

GETAWAYIf you can not stop the rumours, get out of the place, get away from the people who believe the rumours. This is the easiest way to stay away from rumours.

SEARCH FOR If you hear rumours about something other than a person from school or elsewhere, if the rumours are, for example, of a man who died in a house that is believed to be haunted by his spirit, before believing such a story, do your research. See if the incident happened, do not try to stay out of the news too, it is very important.

DICTIONARYIt is very indispensable to use the dictionary when you want to know a word, in case, if you do not know what the word prejudice is, just look up the general meaning of the word in the dictionary.

MEDIA

What is it?

Everyone knows that there are millions of stories about things happening all over the world, but not everything you read or watch can be true. Sometimes people report facts and figures, but other times they opine on those facts and figures, which leads us to misinformation, something that may be or may not be true.

What to do?

Be careful. Do not believe everything you hear. This does not mean you should distrust anyone and think they are lying, that is just being cautious. Learn to differentiate facts and numbers from opinions.

Remember: prejudice occurs when we are in real fact. If we get a lot of opinions, we have enough information to make a good decision, far from prejudice.

PRESSURE AND YOUR TRUE SELF

We have always been looking for an identity to put ourselves in a position, but that does not mean that we should always change our attitude and personality. The difference between pressure and your true self is as follows: Imagine yourself as an intelligent, unpopular, and very rejected person. And then you hear from a person: "You should wear better clothes than what you are wearing, and you should also live life instead of studying."_ Then you look at yourself and say that the other person is talking right, the next day you go dressed differently and change your attitude, then someone comes again and says: "You should eat less, you have a lot of bellies." _ And you look at yourself and agree that you need to work out or eat less.

That is where our history of pressure comes in, it is a waste changing your style on the outside or attitude on the inside because one thing I learned in life was: People will always criticise you for something, no matter where you are or no matter what you are. There will always be someone to criticise you. And now? Well, if you can not look at yourself in the mirror and live happily with who you already are, it means you are not living your true self. To find your true self, here are some tips.

Hobbies

Hobbies are those activities that we always like to do in our daily lives, such as painting, dancing, writing songs, making plays, knitting, embroidering, sewing, playing games, playing sports, and others. It is one of the main ones to start finding your true self. If you like to do some of the things I mentioned, do not change it because that is your true self.

Tastes

Many people prefer to eat only vegetables rather than meat, while others prefer to eat meat rather than some types of vegetables. That is what we are talking about preferences, it does not have to be just about food, sometimes when choosing clothes in a store or setting up a set for a piece. Each will give an opinion on each other's preferences, for example, John says he prefers to wear long clothes in the heat because of the mosquitoes, while Joana says she prefers to wear short clothes because the heat is agonising her. So we have two opinions linked to the use of clothes in the heat. That is, we have two people saying their preferences, and this is also part of our search for the true Self.

Talents

Do you know what talent is? No, talent is not famous people or people who go to Hollywood or Disney to become part of the world of fame and are artists. Talent is something that has been within us since childhood. For

example, my talent has been painting since I was a child. I paint canvases and turn them into something that is part of my personality, my feelings, something I dreamed of, and came true. In your case, the talent could be singing, dancing, acting, decorating, magic, helping other people find themselves, leading a group of people. But be careful, do not confuse the gift with talent, a gift is something that only we can predict, telepathy, something that is difficult for everyone to have. But talent is everything that a person can develop over time.

Culture

The culture of all of us is very different, each country has a specific type of culture, but that does not mean that there will be only that culture there. In the old days, we could say that the culture has been well-preserved on just one base, but now that there have been migrations from all over the place and people moving away from war or looking for another life, many people from foreign origins have come to our continent. Do not worry, tourists can not be counted. To understand what culture is, let us look at the Seven Fine Arts. In each country, there is a type of dance that is unique to them, the most popular are ballroom dancing, ballet, jazz, street dancing, capoeira(Brazil), and tap dancing. And the music we have is electronic, hip hop, classical music, pop, and others. But culture is not just the Seven Fine Arts, even in a country, each state and each region within it will show different cultures. In Brazil, for example, the foods of the Northeast are very different from the foods of the South and Midwest, if you realise, who lives on the coast of the country like San Paulo, Rio de Janeiro, Saint Spirit, and Bahia, the fish they serve on the beach is very different from the fish in Brasilia. And with that, they gain a part of the culture, but if you ask where cheese bread was made, everyone will say that cheese bread was invented in Minas Gerais, which brings us to the culture. If the cheese bread was invented in Minas Gerais, then cheese bread becomes part of the culture, but if a person invents a cheese bread with a different flavour, then this other cheese bread becomes part of the local culture. Above were just a few examples for you to understand what the culture itself is. If your family has an Asian-derived culture, but you are American, that does not mean you should stop following Asian culture, but it also does not mean you should leave your American culture aside and start becoming Asiatic. Do not. Culture is something we follow willingly. I am of

Japanese descent, and I like their culture, but even though I am of Japanese descent, I am also of Brazilian descent, that is, I can live both Brazilian and Japanese culture. This makes us coexist within society as a whole.

Religions

When a person is born, is baptised by the family, and then grows up, he/she is destined to follow a religion, but what if he/she does not want to? Well, a person does not need to follow a religion, there are no laws yet about being obliged to follow a religion. But the one thing that all people must believe is: have a belief in a force greater than ours, believe in him or her. It makes us confident and gives us hopeful, faith. Christians believe in one God, Buddhists believe in Buddha, Indians believe in the holy God, Greeks believe in many gods, and so on. In my case, my family follows the Christian religion, but my family in general, everyone follows a different religion, my father follows spiritualism, my mother is Catholic, my godmother is evangelical, my family living in Japan are Buddhist, my coastal family follows the pagan religion. And how am I? Well, it was very difficult to choose a religion for me, and a lot of people feel the same way, and that is why the first thing everyone should know is to believe in a greater force. Even those who have a religion, or not, suffer prejudice. Because all churches will say something against, for example, the Christian church does not like pagans, evangelicals are Christians, but they do not really believe what Catholics say, spiritualists say one thing and Buddhists say another. Politics is going on between them, even in the songs we sing in the Temple or our Church. But do you want to know our true Church? The true Church is within us, which we call the church or our body temple. And that is why we should respect each other, no matter the religion.

RELEASING THE PRESSURE

Now that you already know what prejudice is, how to find your true self, and also how to know the truth. Release your tensions a little by writing whatever comes to your mind in a state of stress:

Ugh!! Inside I feel like I am screaming:

_______________________ to the people who pressure me.

What drives me crazy is:

____

—

But I also feel:

Anxious/ Confused/ Curious/ Suspicious/ Jealous/ Stereotyped/ Stressed/ Excited/ Frustrated/ Stuck/ Angry / Overwhelmed / Suffocated / Attack

If I give in, I'll probably win:

—

If I give in, I will probably lose:

—

DISORDERS AND WHO CAN HELP

EATING DISORDERS

The moment of truth has arrived. Most people love to eat. This is something they yearn for. A topping sundae is a treat, a Subway sandwich with fries can be the evening snack. But for people with eating disorders, food is the worst enemy. The disorders that I will mention are serious and this can get even worse if the person does not adjust, especially the girls who say they want to lose their belly or weight. Most eating disorders seem really normal. You can not just tell by what people say or walk. Some people suffer from bulimia (binge) and anorexia.

People who suffer from a bulimia eating disorder are people who do not stop eating and can only stop when it is time to put everything out, a custom of the ancient Romans. Those who suffer from anorexia are people who will probably skip meals and start exercising, thus, they end up missing important meals of the day, and instead of eating what is essential, the person ends up eating less than they should. Later they will be able to faint. People keep secrets. We always have a system for transmitting messages, who has not written in a diary? And we use nicknames to chat with other people online in secret. Girls have excellent secret-keeping skills, of course, when we get nervous we end up talking nonsense, and at the same time, we accidentally spill a secret. You may become suspicious of people who have an eating disorder, you try to talk to him/her about it, but he/she immediately changes the subject. Everything indicates that he/she suffers from an eating disorder, a person who does not have an eating disorder would calmly talk about it.

Eating disorders that people have

Anorexia nervosa

Usually, girls are the ones who have anorexia nervosa the most, boys not so much. People who have this disorder: The organisation of Anorexia Nervosa and Related Eating Disorders (ANRED- Anorexia Nervosa and Relationship of Eating Disorders) reports that one out of one hundred girls between the ages of ten and twenty starve to death.

People say this is because:

I am slimming.

I have control over my body.

I am doing everything the way it should be done.

I command myself.

Other people have noticed that I:

I skip all or half of my meals.

I started to develop soft, white hairs on my face and neck.

I want to exercise all the time.

I cut my food into small pieces and shove it onto my plate.

I have multiple food rituals, like chewing a certain number of times before swallowing.

I do not tell it, because:

This is not a serious thing and I can handle it.

I do not want to worry anyone

I don not want to look stupid, like I made a mistake.

Everything is almost perfect, and I do not want to stop so close to my goals.

Other people do not need to know what is going on in life.

Where to get help:

Eating Disorders Support and Treatment Group Bulimia and Eating Disorders

Outpatient Clinic of the Institute of Psychiatry, Hospital, Faculty of Medicine Study Group on Nutrition and Eating Disorders

Guidance and Assistance Program for Patients with Eating Disorders

Bulimia nervosa

Like people with anorexia nervosa, most victims are also girls. People who have this disorder: ANRED reports that four out of one hundred school-age girls suffer from bulimia. For teenage girls, the number is difficult to calculate because those with anorexia may also be bulimic or develop bulimia later.

People say this is because:

I have my secrets

I can control my body's appearance

I can release my stress

I am doing everything the way it should be done

I command myself

Other people have noticed that I:

I look really strange

I go to the bathroom after meals

I take a lot of medicine like laxatives

I have binge attacks or I exercise compulsively

I do not tell it, because:

This is nothing serious and I can handle it

I do not want people to know that I am thin because I am bulimic.

Everything is almost perfect, and I do not want to stop so close to my goals.

Other people do not need to know what is going on in my life

Where to get help:

Search for help for anorexia, already cited. Centres that treat girls who are anorexic also treat bulimic girls. Below I show the organisation of the food pyramid. These foods are delicious, but in excess, they can mean health problems and even a few extra pounds, but it does not mean you can not eat it.

The first level of the food pyramid is known for cereals and carbohydrates (rice, bread, pasta), which should be consumed in greater quantities, as they are sources of energy.

The second level corresponds to fruits and salads that help replenish vitamins and minerals.

The third level is the group of white and red meats, milk, which help in the development and growth of the body.

The fourth level is composed of sugars, sweets, oils, fats, which we can eat, but without overdoing it.

But if you do not want snacks and quick meals, they can be replaced with pieces of cheese and crackers without filling.

MENTAL DISORDERS

When you get sick, it is usually something that is here now but will be gone tomorrow, like when you catch a cold or the flu. It is not that big of a problem, and you recover quickly. Mental illness is a lot like that, except you do not recover that quickly. People can have issues that last for years instead of just a few days or weeks. And what makes the situation even worse is that sometimes you do not even know if a person is sick. A person who is depressed may feel sad inside, but maintain an expression of happiness for everyone who sees him/her. If so, nothing seems strange when people talk to him/her. They think the boy/girl is fine, but he/she knows he/she is terrible. This is the similarity between eating disorders and mental disorders. But the difference between them is that the mental disorder lasts longer than the eating disorder. The longer they linger in your head, the worse you get overtime.

1.   *You may lose the love you have for yourself as a person.*

2.   *You may lose the ability to dream, be inspired, or feel the power of God in your life.*

3.   *You may lose faith in your abilities, and you may lose touch with the people who are close to you. Nothing is worth it. But it is a difficult thing to realise if you already suffer from depression, addiction, or some form of injury, such as self-harm.*

1.   *If you already have a mental disorder, it can be hard to say, enough, I will end it! And just walk away. Instead of thinking of mental disorders as something that just will not exist in your life anymore, let us talk about this in more detail.*

DEPRESSION

Depression has its levels, there is a low depression where the individual is depressed by something he wanted, but did not happen. There is an intermediate depression, where the individual thinks more than he should and feels down about something that bothers him. And there is the most dangerous depression of all, which is when the individual thinks that everything around him is a disaster, tragedy, and suffering, leading him to take dangerous attitudes and walk to death. People who have this disorder: The American Academy of Child and Adolescent Psychiatry reports that depression is something that happens to many people. About 5% of children and teens deal with depression, and many adults do as well.

People say this is because:

I do not work anymore

I do not care about anything

I never feel like getting up, going out, or doing anything.

I am sad, but I do not know why.

Other people have noticed that I:

I have withdrawn from my friends and spent time alone.

I get sad very quickly and even cry a lot.

I am in a bad mood

I sleep or eat a lot

I do not tell it, because:

I can not figure out what is wrong.

I am too tired to take this seriously.

Nobody can do anything anyway.

Where to get help:

narcotics centre (if you are addicted to drugs)

psychiatrist (if you are addicted to something, it does not need to be just because of drugs)

psychologist (if you are hurt, with mental health broke)

CUTS OR SELF-HARM

People who do this tend to do worse things that involve cutting and cutting and self-harming. Self-harm is not an insignificant disorder. The Rutgers University Family Education Network reported that the number of people who self-harm have approached three million. Half or more of these people are girls who are either stimulated by their negative feelings or forced by terrorists and other bad people.

People say this is because:

I can not get my feelings out.

This is my private secret.

There is a lot of pressure in my life.

I can release all my stress.

Other people have noticed that I:

I can not talk about my feelings.

I started wearing long clothes, even in hot weather.

I am moody and I am constantly angry.

I can not take things very well.

I do not tell it, because:

I deserve what I am doing to myself.

People would find it totally absurd

I need to free myself

Where to get help:

psychiatrist (if you are doing it because it feels fine and normal)

psychologist (if you are hurt, think others will notice you are their failure)

SUICIDE

The first thing people think about is this and that is why they start to self-mutilate, cut themselves, threaten others saying they are going to kill themselves because the world is cruel, and they do not accept you for what you are, that you are evil. The people who do it: The Journal of the American Medical Association (JAMA) published an article saying that suicide is the third leading killer of people between the ages of 15 and 24. The article also says that although boys commit more suicides than girls, girls think about and attempt to commit suicide more often than boys. And some movies and series also influence many young people and adults to tragically and unintentionally commit suicide.

People say this is because:

There is no more hope.

I can control the situation

Nobody cares about me

People would be better off without me

Other people have noticed that I:

I have big mood swings.

I withdraw from people and spend time alone.

I criticise myself a lot.

I started talking about death.

I do not tell it, because:

I do not think anyone really cares

Not worth the effort.

Nobody would do anything anyway.

Where to get help:

psychiatrist (if you are doing it because it feels fine and normal to think about it)

psychologist (if you are hurt, think others will notice you are their failure)

ADDICTION (Cigarette, Alcohol and Drugs)

It is no wonder that drugs are what people use the most, some say it is to calm and help with stress, others say they help you lose weight, that it cures any disease, that it helps you see things we do not see when we are conscious. Many American films also force many of the young actors and actresses to use real drugs in multiple scenes(takes) in the film, even those in which there is no pornography or anything like that. Another reason is the influence of adults on young people, young people think that using drugs makes them adults and part of society. Others want to experiment to see what effect and how it feels on them, or when they are very depressed and want to be even more depressed.

But does it really cause all this? Do drugs really help your health, your emotions, your growth, your life? The people who do it: Since research done by the Centre for Addiction and Substance Abuse in 2003, CASA has reported that girls are now on par with boys when it comes to alcohol and drug addiction. But unlike boys, girls become addicts earlier. They also start to get sick more easily when using drugs and alcohol frequently.

People say this is because:

I am just having fun, this is nothing serious.

Everyone experiences things when they get to my age. (16,17,18 years old)

I am not addicted because I am going to stop soon. (But NO)

It makes me look like an adult.

Other people have noticed that I:

I have trouble paying attention and concentrating.

I spend a lot of extra money.

I have new friends who do not seem trustworthy or are older.

I have reddened or sleepy, tired eyes that seem distant.

I smell like cigarette smoke or alcohol, even when I am wearing perfume, cologne, or deodorant.

I do not tell it, because:

I do not have a problem

This is not a serious thing

I am planning to stop

I do not want anyone to know what is going on

I can not stop because I owe people money

Where to get help:

psychiatrist (if you are addicted to something, it does not need to be just because of drugs)

psychologist (if you are hurt, think others will notice you are their failure, if you are hurt, with mental health broke)

narcotics centre

GETTING HELP AND RECOVERING YOURSELF

There are four people who can help you. Your <u>parents,</u> <u>Support Agencies, Psychologists</u>, and <u>Psychiatrists</u>. First, let us talk a little about the role that each one performs.

Parents: They are responsible for the house, the people who give us clothes, toys, materials, pay for electricity and water so that we can live with light(energy) and water without having to worry about hygiene(cleaning), such as cooking and others. They also brought you into this world, and it is their duty to educate you all.

Now, if you are adopted, try to ask questions to yourself:

- *They adopted me when I was a baby or as a child?*

- *Was it worthy to be alone in the world without a home, food and a place to entertain myself?*

- *Do I have friends helping me?*

- *Are my parents(biological or adopted) taking care of me in the right way or is it me complaining that I do not have everything I want?*

- *Can I eat, sleep, play and go to school(learn)?*

Support Agencies: They only deal with one problem, if, for example, you have disorders, as we said before, you can seek help with the centres I had mentioned. They are considered the supporting agencies. So do not even think that they will help you with difficulties at home, the only ones that can help you more with family issues and others are the two below.

Psychologists: Psychologists are like our diary, in our diary we write everything that comes to mind or depending on our deepest feelings, a friend we can trust. The psychologist is the same thing, he/she is our doctor, and friend. The psychologist is a doctor of the mind, he/she takes care of the health of our head and shows us solutions on how to solve the problems we face on a daily basis. He/She is our friend in the literary sense, but he/she is a person we can trust, do not be afraid to tell him/her what you are feeling and why you are feeling it. And he/she is also our doctor. I remember the psychologist I had, she really cured me and I saw that the problems in the family were in the part of getting the whole family together and talking calmly.

Psychiatrists: Psychiatrists are like psychologists, but the difference is that they are like doctors who prescribe medication. Well, if you say the following: "Doctor, I'm not feeling very close to my family, I think I'm going to commit suicide." At the same time, the psychiatrist will tell you: "Take this prescription, buy this medicine and take it twice a day." In my opinion, start by asking the parents for help, but if you can not, go to the agencies, and if they charge the price of a psychologist, go to the psychologist. Psychiatrists only in worse cases.

I will ask you four questions, answer me in the lines below what you think of each of the names I mentioned earlier of the people who can help you with difficult issues of your daily routine.

Who are they?(parents/ support agencies/ psychologists/ psychiatrists) (Remember to mention all of them).

____

____

____

____

____

____

____

____

____

____

____

____

____

____

____

Why can they help you (parents/ support agencies/ psychologists/ psychiatrists)?(Remember to talk about all of them).

____

____

____

____

____

____

____

____

____

____

____

____

____

____

____

____

How do you make them listen to you? (parents/support agencies/psychologists/psychiatrists)?(Remember to talk about all of them).

____

____

____

____

____

____

____

Who will know about it? (parents/ support agencies/ psychologists/ psychiatrists)?(Remember to talk about all of them).

Was it difficult to answer these questions? If so, great, because here it is a basic explanation for all the questions. When I asked who they are in the sense of all of them, it means the following, for us to understand better, let me explain in parts:

Parents: Would you define the word parents as those who made you appear in this world, known as father and mother? But your "father" and your "mother" can also be an uncle, aunt, grandmother, grandfather, relatives, and any responsible person who takes care of you, but does not repress or attack you all the time.

Support Agencies: They are groups of people who run clinics or support centres simply because they want to help. We have, for example, the Guardianship Council for children and teenagers. When they suffer from some type of violence, changes in behaviour, and more serious cases, the agencies can help.

Psychologists: Psychologists are specialists who help all of us understand what is wrong with our minds.

Psychiatrists: Unlike psychologists, psychiatrists study medical school and become doctors. They help all of us to understand what is wrong with our minds and body.

Why can they help you?

Parents: They know you, and that is why they should help you, however, it is important to know that your parents love you, we do not want to see aggressive parents.

Support Agencies: They help you with a specific type of problem. To be clearer, I will explain how this works: Imagine you are having concerns with addictions, you look for an agency that takes care of this specific type of issue, and they help you.

Psychologists: Psychologists were once people who suffered difficulties in adolescence and as a child, but they also understand everything when it comes to a concern inside our head. They are people who graduated from the faculty of psychology, and that is why it is significant to hear what they can say to help us understand and try to get closer to people.

Psychiatrists: Psychiatrists are doctors who generate revenue if the patient needs it, he/she is not the same as the psychologist, but it is as if it were. They can help you in more serious cases that are about your body and mind. They may or may not generate prescriptions for you to take medicine, depending on how you describe your problems.

How do you make them listen to you?

Parents: Sometimes I know it is difficult for them to understand us. Think that they were once children and teenagers and went through more difficult things than they are now. To make them listen to you, organise a family time when you and your parents can talk smoothly and without interruptions.

Support Agencies: They will only assist you if you look for the agency online and then call their number, so a suitable person will answer your problems.

Psychologists: Usually, in schools, there is a psychologist to help students. You can email them and ask for help with an issue, but if there is no psychologist in your school, another way is to look for one in the telephone directories or in advertisements on the websites.

Psychiatrists: Psychiatrists are doctors, so like all other areas of medicine, you should make an appointment first, so you can talk to them. So, after making the appointment, you can talk to him about your physical and mental disorders. Depending on your age, your parents will have to go along.

Who will know about it?

Parents: Only them. Unless there is someone spying on you or nearby.

Support Agencies: The support agency may contact your parents, a doctor, or other people who may be able to help you.

Psychologists: If you are going to a school psychologist, your conversation with him or her will be kept confidential, but if you are going to an outside psychologist, he/she may tell your parents something. Unless you have booked it for yourself only. By law it is important to keep confidential, after all, it is about your private emotions and life.

Psychiatrists: In the case of psychiatrists, they will give you the prescription, so when you show the prescription to the pharmacies, the pharmacists will know about the medicine you take, but they will not go into more details.

Body

BEAUTY

This is the hardest part for us to define for people. Appearance does matter, but what about when it comes to inner beauty? When you are young, appearance is very important, but we live in a real-world, get out of the world of princes and princesses. The world can be shallow, confusing and a source of stress when it comes to beauty. Girls are increasingly striving to change their appearance by doing plastic surgery, putting on makeup because they are sure they will feel safer. As for the boys, some do plastic surgery, others put on lenses that change the colour of their eyes, and use anabolic steroids. And do you know why they do it? We are going to find out in this chapter.

In the 11th century, that is, between the years 1100 and 1300, beauty was the infallible tool to differentiate poor, rich, gentle, and evil people. That is why, when we see someone wearing dirty clothes and with an ugly face, we already think they are poor and ridiculous, but when the person is all dressed up, with a beautiful face and walking elegantly, we already see that they are rich. But what if suddenly they are nothing like what they are wearing? And that is where the beauty issues come in.

The peculiarities of outer beauty

The fact is this: Looking good, however you define beauty, can give us a powerful feeling of glamour that lifts us and makes us feel like we have a million dollars. Imagine that you are a girl who likes to always change your look, so you put on makeup in as many ways as possible, about to come out all pretty. You go to meet your friends, start chatting about funny things, and suddenly a friend of yours throws water in your face without meaning to or on purpose. That is it, the clowning is over, he/she squirted or splashed water on your face and smeared all the perfect makeup you had done to attract the attention of the boy/girl you like. Know that in situations like this, only the outer beauty is spoiled, but our inner beauty will always be the same. And I am not talking about biology, I am talking about our emotions. We are talking about the body in this chapter, but if you want to talk about the mind again, read chapter one.

Skin

Teenagers' struggle for skin is so dramatic that sometimes even a soap opera can not compete. Some talk about worries about pimples, blemishes, dirt, wrinkles. Clean skin is the result of cleaning(washing), unobstructed pores. When you have acne, it is a sign that you have clogged pores on your skin. So anywhere you have skin, even on your buttocks, you can have acne. There are chances of having dead skin clogging your pores, but there is a sebum oil that helps to unclog your pores. The difference between yellow head acne and blackhead acne is as follows:

- **Yellowhead acne:**The clogged pore received bacteria inside it and closed.

- **Blackhead acne:**The clogged pore remained open and got dirt on it.

- **Pimple:**The clogged pore closes and swells under the skin.

Advice: Keep your hands off and your skin clean. Daily, get into the regular habit of cleaning your skin. Wash it, do not use a rough sponge or exfoliating. Use a damp cotton ball or a face cloth as an astringent to remove dirt from your skin. You can buy an astringent at the pharmacy, but remember, after you remove dirt from your skin with the astringent, immediately apply a facial moisturiser. And finally, your skin will not look beautiful just by cleaning it with astringents and other acne and pimple products. You should also keep your skin hydrated, so drink water.

When it comes to odour, everyone knows what to do. Every day, on sunny days or hot days, our body starts to sweat, this happens because our body is releasing the water that it had kept inside the body and is now being thrown out of the body to cool off. It is like taking a shower, but it is very agonising because of the smell that comes with it, we all know it as "BS(body smell)". I am going to show you two basic ideas that you might find useful.

First: Buy a deodorant and every three hours, apply it to the place where your body is sweating. Deodorant does not stop sweat, but it will eliminate the agonising odour that was in the air. If that does not work, apply lemon under your armpit daily, so the smell does not get worse(but if you use lemon, do not go outside to sunbathe).

Second: Try to wear cotton clothes, including underwear. Clothes made of synthetic material do not let in enough air for your skin to breathe.

HAIR

Hair is also part of our puzzle, it is what makes us crazy and crazy to go to the salon, no matter what kind of hair or what hair (eyebrows, fur, beard, moustache). Before you are sure you are going to cut your hair, take it easy, do not cut 15 centimetres of your hair yet, it is best to take it easy. Because as soon as you cut your hair for the first time, and you end up not liking it, you regret it and try to go back in time (but you can not anymore because you already cut it, and now you must leave it as is). It is always good to experiment with different styles or colours on your hair, but dye spoils your hair, as does a flat iron and dryer is too hot and can weaken your hair. All of them will dehydrate your hair and over time can become oily or very dry, the same goes for the type of shampoo and conditioner that each one uses, do not use a shampoo that is not appropriate for your hair type.

Another important tip is to let your hair air dry, first, you remove excess water from your hair with your hand after showering, then you dry it with a towel and then let it dry naturally. Wrapping the towel around your head also damages your hair, and over time it can become dry and greasy.

MAKEUP

There are myths and truths about how to use makeup correctly, but makeup is where most girls make mistakes and make mistakes. Many girls think that makeup products will make them look older. This method can work if it's done by a professional makeup artist, but for an average girl, the makeup can go down to being a totally circus-like clown. Here I will show you just a few tips, so you don't make more mistakes.

1. *Using wet eyeshadow to intensify the shade more is a myth, you can not make art with makeup on your face as if it is painted, wetting it indeed gives a more intensified tone.*

2. *Avon's BB cream makeup serves as a quick base, the right thing is to match your skin tone and start hiding blackheads and pimples.*

3. *If you do not buy branded products, but you have lipstick and lip gloss at home, do the following; on the lips, apply your lipstick, and do not dry out your mouth, apply four touches of lip gloss. So your mouth is perfect and shiny.*

4. *The brown eyebrow pencil is the basis for grooming your eyebrows, but it will not always be ideal and appropriate for your eyebrows.*

5. *Always keep makeup tools clean (brushes, sponges, others). To avoid picking up bacteria.*

1. **The tip is:**Do not wet the eyeshadow, instead, take the brush, wet the tip of the brush, and apply the eyeshadow. Even because, when the eyeshadow is wet, it picks up germs and bacteria over time, and this can ruin your skin.

2. **The tip is:**Choose the makeup according to your skin tone and make circular designs on the cheekbones, forehead, and chin. Then spread it well with your fingers in circular motions all over your face. The main parts are below the eyes, the eyelids, the forehead, the cheekbones, the chin, below the nose, and a little on the top of the nose. Spread it well, you can get a good result and manage to hide the pimples.

3. **The tip is:**Exactly what it says above, and remember to choose one of the two if you want to use only one. The lipstick leaves a more vibrant tone, even the lighter ones, since the shine it hydrates, but if you use it too much it runs off and also leaves a feeling of something sticky on your lips.

4. **The tip is:**It is not always necessary to fix the eyebrows, the Japanese do the eyebrows directly because they shave the eyebrow hairs and in its

place, they draw the shape of eyebrows they want. If you have a deformed eyebrow or want to change its shape, it is best to look for a professional to draw your eyebrows for you.

5. **The tip is:**Who just keeps makeup tools without cleaning them, over time they pick up bacteria that came from the air itself or your face when it is not clean. And it can spoil your skin. Try to buy new tools.

For you girls, makeup must be innovated <u>every season of the year.</u>This helps to make you more confident. Makeup expresses who you are, but it does not define you. To finish the subject about beauty and makeup, let us review what we learned: Your appearance matters. But that is not all. Outer beauty is a tool at your disposal, not a prison in which you have to live up to a standard that has been set too high. Becoming mature means accepting external beauty problems, such as pimples and acne marks, as part of your growing body. Hair and makeup can reflect who we are inside. We can use them to express how we change, mature, and grow. Our look is an expression of who we are, not the definition of who we are. Being beautiful on the outside is great, but what matters is our inner well-being.

FASHION

Fashion is a fun way to show our personality to the world. Whatever our style, remember that fashion is not just clothes and accessories, we also have job styles (architecture, automobiles, others). Time to go out somewhere, or time to have a nap. We will always be dressing differently. A lot of people even at bedtime wear fancy clothes to sleep, which we call sleep fashion. Even in fashion, girls and guys are desperate about what to wear. But looking at it the other way around, here are three good things that fashion can do for you:

- *It can help you to play the role you will play in life. (when you go to a job interview, for example.)*

- *It can help you with a million different choices for each case. (You are dressing to go out and have two shirts; blue and red to wear with a pair of pants.)*

- *It can be replaced in a second. Tired of a look or want a change? No problem, because fashion can be replaced. (You are hippie, but now you want to try the gothic look)*

What matters: Mind, heart, soul

The best clothes in the world are nothing but cheap packaging. Learning this lesson now will only help you as you grow, mature, and experience navigating the world of fashion. In your mind, you think that fashion is something that can save you from something, but in your heart, you are just feeling how beautiful or perfect you are. But in your soul, you think and feel that in some cases fashion will not always comfort you.

Soul

FAMILY

The family is our support system, an enthusiasm section, and a safety net. There will always be, in a family, someone in charge. Family is care, protection, and concern. The family respects its space, but it always has a good side and a bad side.

The good side

A good family times are probably the things you remember most, think about where your family keeps the old family album photos. Now that you're thinking about your family's photo collection, do the following: Get up and grab a family album to remember the times you spent together with them, and if so, see if there are any photos of the kids. Right now, you may not have the family photo album on your lap, but you continue to read this book. The intention of making you pick up the family album is the following, just like when we watch a film on television or on the computer, movies cause us a kind of empathy, the same happens when we look at something and remember the moment. For them, we have three questions and four important feelings; Inspiration, love, affection, and support.

What it is?

Inspiration: This is the feeling your family has among everyone when it comes to supporting each other.

Love: Love is the feeling you get when you do anything for someone, always supporting and helping you to your best.

Support: Support is listening, encouraging, caring, and believing in the people you interact with.

Affection: Physical affection is helping or hugging. Emotional affection is being there, no matter the occasion.

Why does it matter?

Inspiration: We have to take steps towards bigger and better things. We need to look at each other to grow. Without inspiration, you have no one to accompany you on your journey.

Love: Love makes your soul grow. Without it, you lose hope in all sorts of things in life.

Support: Support is what guarantees that you will be able to fulfil the goals that will make you a better person. It is the guide and balance for those moments when you are feeling lost.

Affection: Affection gives you that feeling that everything is going to be okay. It makes us feel that we will always have a safe haven.

Managing it

Inspiration: To get the most inspiration, look at people's weaknesses and strengths, especially in your family.
Love: Generate love from small gestures and small things to the biggest ones. This is the way to generate love on all sides of the equation.
Support: The key to support is establishing a balance and identifying where and when people need support.
Affection: Affection can be a one-way street.

Despite everything, there are always people in our lives who make an impact. We may even think that we never had people important to us, or even that we didn't strengthen very strong bonds. Quite the opposite. There is always someone marking us, in the best way. These people are rare, but they do exist. I was lucky to have one of them who knew how to give the true value that may be very few people, or almost no one, gave me. Your words and gestures are kept, and I thank you every day for having a friend so close to me in special and difficult times. In life, we meet a lot of nice people, but we also meet a lot of boring people. To know which side you are on, the first thing is to organize your mind, you can retake the tests from chapter one. But here we are talking about your soul, there are methods of cleansing the soul in order to remove bad things, have you ever heard of good karma and bad karma? That's exactly it. We've already talked about the good side of being within a family, but now let's see the bad side.

The bad side

Your family's downswings can range from small fights between brothers and sisters to wide-ranging family battles. Sometimes bad times separate families for a short time. Other times, what goes wrong can tear a family apart forever. Who has never tried to break up the fight between father and mother when one of the two was doing something wrong? Or who has never felt guilty and already wanted to commit suicide, thinking it was the children's fault and not the parents? I admit that this has happened to me several times, even though my parents are separated, we are still a happy family, but when I was a child I already threatened to kill myself in front of the two of them. For better reflection, we can go back to chapter one to talk about mental disorders again. But to get into the subject, for now, let's continue reading below. Within a family, we find many feelings, but the most common among them all is guilt, anxiety, distrust, and anger. The most negative and bad feelings when we are living with the bad side of families.

What it is?

Guilt: Guilt is a type of regret. You usually feel guilty about something you did wrong. This can be established for a long time and turned into a constant problem.

Anxiety: Anxiety is the result of worrying about nervousness. What makes you feel insecure and leads to a lack of self-confidence.

Distrust: Each family keeps secrets, things the members are not proud of.

Anger: Some families struggle with a lot of anger, such as screaming, violence, or abuse. Others fight with hidden anger, such as resentment, hatred, or disapproval.

Why are they important?

Guilt: Guilt can show you were wrong. But you can feel guilty if you didn't do anything wrong. This is the guilt trip that families sometimes put on their members.

Anxiety: Anxiety can paralyse anyone. Constant worrying about what to do can leave you feeling helpless. It is essential to make sure that anxiety does not override your own will about your role within the family.

Distrust: Distrust destroys trust between people, and when this occurs within families, the lines of communication are totally interrupted. Without a way to communicate, families begin to fall apart.

Anger: Anger is the quickest way to make situations between families worse. This occurs after rewinding the state of affairs. Finding a place on the lines of communication can be difficult and resentments can grow.

Managing it

Guilt: Guilt must be managed by the mind and actions. Find out if the feeling of guilt is justifiable or not. Then work on that part to confront things that need to be changed.

Anxiety: When you are anxious, you feel as if your brain itself works exhaustively to imagine the worst. So, to control anxiety, you need to take a deep breath and calm down.

Distrust: Managing distrust is something very difficult to do. Once a family member loses another person's trust, it's pretty hard to have chances for other people involved. But you must find a way to rebuild trust.

Anger: This kind of feeling is manageable, no matter what people say. People have control over their reactions and can take a step back when things get close to exploding.

The ugly side

Now we come back to the worst part: abuse and dysfunction. Although the families have broken lines of communication and fight with each other, some have sexually inappropriate, violent behaviour and abuse the laws of the Statutes. If you live in a family that is physically or sexually abusive, this can be scary. When people are constantly afraid of being hurt, attacked, beaten, physically punished, or touched in a sexually inappropriate way, their bodies and mind are always tense. It's a jittery feeling high in your stomach that never goes away. Most of these people are constantly living in absolute fear. They fear being abused. They fear other family members who are being abused. Not only that, but they fear that people outside the family will find out what is going on. Abuse is almost always a secret. And well, you're not alone, because, in 2001, the US Department of Health and Social Services counted all cases of abused children in 2001, found that about 13 children out of 1,000 families were abused. And in 2009, the US Department of Health and Social Services compared child sexual abuse in Brazil with children in North America. Both are totally violable. To prevent this from happening, it's always good to have an adult we can trust, if you don't have a trusted adult, call a centre that helps people in this situation. Also, call toll-free, abuse is an emergency to report the abuse of children, women, and girls.

FRIENDSHIP

Friendship is not just in school, college, or olden times. Friendship can be found through small gestures too. Is that what friends are for? Have you heard the question above? If so, think for a moment and discuss the word "friendship". During adolescence, girls and boys need friends more than ever. In friendship, we keep centred, share dreams, encourage each other to reach the goal, show a way out to solve problems, and make the good times even better. Friends will always be there in different cases. But there's no guarantee about friendships. Not everyone is nice, and that's why you need to understand that there are different types of friends. The friend and the hobby friend Hobby friends are people we meet because we run in similar circles. A friend or hobby friend is someone who plays the same sport as you, a person you meeting, every Sunday at church, or someone who works with us.

There are bad things and there are good things in terms of friends-hobbies. The good part is that you usually don't expect to argue or have serious fights with a hobby friend. In this case, hobbies are not our disposable handkerchiefs (people who help us through difficult times), they don't have to deal with us when things go bad. It's hard to say who's doing what's really going on, because we've only seen each other for a short while. There's always an exception to every rule, isn't there? In this case, the exception may be a hobby that takes up a reasonable amount of time in your daily life. The friends need to see each other in weekly training sessions. Be on the lookout for friends-hobbies that may appear in your everyday life.

The stalker friend Have you ever had someone following your every step? This is absolutely horrible. It's like you're being followed and spied on by an evil agency. But let's not get into fantasy right now, let's suppose you go to your locker at school and that person you don't even know or like is there. At first, you act naturally as if nothing is happening, but the moment you go to the cafeteria, there is the person again, at the bus stop, there is also that person again. This leads us to a very big coincidence, either you are being spied on or you are being stalked. So here's the worst part, someone has to tell that person the truth, in case you. Don't feel bad if you don't feel that friendly vibe with someone hanging on to you. God created each person as a single individual. But to better understand the question of friendship, let's see if you really have a true friendship or is it just another illusion.

FRIENDSHIP QUIZ

Here, you will ask yourself these questions and answer them honestly.

- Can I ask my friends and really get an honest answer?

- Do people think I'm FAT?

- What do I hope to become or do in the future with my life?

- What am I best at?

- Am I annoying sometimes?

The first solution to find out the answer is: First, research what you already know from your friends like favourite food, sports, or clothes. Then ask them and see if the answer is fair.

For example, I know a friend of mine who likes to draw a lot, but even though she likes it, she always says that she prefers trouble to drawing for a boy who only makes trouble at school. One day I asked her if she liked to draw, and she said no, but these days I saw her in front of her house drawing. That's when I realized she wasn't really a friend of mine at all, if she was, she would have been honest with me.

The four things that make a friendship true are: Confidence about what we hear or see around us in life. An ear to hear each other's dreams and know what's inside the soul. An inspiring eye to find what's inside you. An opening to be able to be absolutely honest with each other.

Who will you choose to be? Now that you've learned a lot about yourself and life, say who you will choose to be below:

____

____

____

____

____

____

____

____

____

____

____

____

____

Education and psychoanalysis

PLAYING IN PSYCHOANALYSIS

The English analyst Donald Woods Winnicott was born in Plymouth in 1896 and died in London in 1971. He studied medicine, and his first year of college coincided with the beginning of the First World War. At that time, he even joined the Navy as a trainee surgeon. After the war ended, Winnicott continued his medical training in London. In 1923, at the age of 27, he had his first post as a paediatrician in a hospital. He started the private medical practice, got married on his first marriage, and started the first analysis that lasted ten years. Despite his clinical practice as a paediatrician having begun before his activities as a psychoanalyst, his interest in Psychoanalysis was awakened even before his entry into paediatrics. According to Claire Winnicott, his second wife, two main reasons led Winnicott to pediatrics: admiration he had for a famous paediatrician of the time and the desire to do an analysis, which would only be possible in London. For a time, Winnicott was a singular case in medicine. He was a paediatrician in analytical training. The cultural roots of his thinking were undoubtedly embedded in the psychoanalytic thinking of the time. The relationship of his ideas with the theories of Freud and Melanie Klein is evident but in a particular and creative way. Winnicott was an innovative person. For him, creativity was precisely in the process of destroying and recreating objects. Thus, he used the metaphor of the baby with the mother's breast to propose that the destruction of the breast object, in fantasy, precedes the creative use of objects. With Psychoanalysis, he did no different: he recreated existing concepts, which in his imagination he had already destroyed. The constitution of the subject at the time of play is that he also has this essential characteristic of human creativity, which is to create, destroy and recreate the objects and relationships that are around us. Through playing, the child tries to understand the world around him, providing conditions that facilitate his motor development, his constitution as a subject, his social relationships and his learning. Motor development is understood here as the unfolding of motor and physiological functions. For such development, it is necessary, first, to constitute a subject.

As stated by Levin (1997), and according to Psychoanalysis, there is no development equal to the other. For all development, first, a subjective structure is needed that supports the physical-motor development, making each subject unique. As Mrech says; *"There is no development equal to the other, whether physical, social or emotional. The maturational processes of a child are discrepant in relation to the others. Its structure is always unique, following the specific processes, linked to the history of each subject"*. The play suggested by Kupfer, when he says that:

"The entry of the subject, determined by a very particular story, the effect of his encounter

with language,makes us think about the need to focus on each child, in an attempt to

accompany by them their peculiar way of learning or not learning. (Kupfer, 2001, p.128)"

Nowadays, society exerts too much authority over a child too much and causes early full-grown, that is, children live with a busy schedule and don't have time to play or relax. Even low-income children who study in public schools are also involved in some way by this social demand to produce and succeed. Even if they are not able to attend English, computer, or sports classes, the social discourse also affects them, in the demands of parents and teachers, pressing them to respond to the expectations of a given society. That way, they also don't have much time to play or do other activities that give them pleasure.

Schools also resist balancing pedagogical activities with the positive gains from play. Within the formal tradition of curricula, the school devalues play. Many educators believe that the programs to be fulfilled must be fixed and follow a certain order. The programs ignore the experience that the child is experiencing and, according to Alves (2001), teachers uselessly try to produce life and interest from them. The students' lack of interest in school largely stems from this, as school education, in the given programs, does not correspond to the child's life experience.

Playing is not a silly way for the child to be distracted, to pass the time. The Dutch historian Johan Huizinga (1872-1945) coined the expression Homo Ludens (the man who plays). According to this historian, the notion of play has influenced all great human achievements. From the child in the mother's womb to the child outside the mother, they begin to play their first games, thus, a symbolic world begins. The child in the womb responds with kicks to the mother's caresses, the child outside the mother and with the first years of life, learns to speak a few words, exercises babbling and words explores the corners of the house, plays hide-and-seek, shoots objects to the floor, all this representing the symbolic world.

The representation of social roles is also remarkable, usually, the girl is mirrored in the mother, and the boy is inspired by the father. Winnicott (1975, p.79) stated in his book Playing and Reality that: "*it is in playing, and perhaps only in playing, that the child or adult enjoys their creative freedom.*" The author states that the adult brings with it anxieties, investments, fantasies, the knowledge that will be transferred, in part, to the relationship with the child. It is known that we apprehend childhood from our own. Today, there is a great need to recover the games of the past, those with which previous generations - our grandparents and our parents - played. Psychoanalysis points to the importance of recognizing and rescuing the roots of the human psyche. Our day-to-day practice is always filled with our life stories, by the social, by the culture. Recovering our cultural wealth would contribute substantially to the educational process, in addition to promoting a movement of appropriation of children's roots, which is of paramount psychic importance. In the same line of thought, Sayão says that:

"Teaching means recreating the possibility of observing life from the narrative of

the ancestors, in the form of thecultural legacy. And the institution of looking at

humanexperience is today, par excellence, the school."(Sayao,2004, p.57)

The rescue of traditional children's games enables the construction and reconstruction of individual and collective identity. As well as things that are already very ready, toys that are very sophisticated and industrialized are not as instigators of creation. The loss of previous experience, of the possibility of reflection, of memory as a support for the construction of identity, cultural rooting, and participation in the collective, a result of current modernization, meant the advent of a subject without memory, without ties to tradition, without the possibility of reflection.

To better understand what I meant by the loss of previous experience, just observe, today we are in the Third Industrial Revolution, soon we will be in the fourth, but even now, children are already connected with playing in electronics. They forget the real world and stay tuned in to their electronic devices, few play board games or talk to their colleagues, this happens because we are losing our cultural identity. In the old days, when television did not exist, there were more children who played in the streets, who invented games, who sought to meet in a place to start a game. But now that we have technology, it is not so difficult to communicate with people from afar, but they are causing our society to lose cultural identity.

The freedom of creation is related to some aspect of children's creativity, with the possibility for the child to enter the world of language and be able to make a personal mark of it, with their own style. The child manages to establish a creative relationship with the world, becoming, over time, able to use what has been discovered by him.

To face the challenges of modernity and take advantage of the possibilities that exist, the world needs people who think creatively, who know how to use the information they receive in schools, universities (colleges) on a daily basis, but from new points of view. The fact that something is always being done in the same way does not guarantee that it can think differently, can innovate.

We human beings always try to modify reality to obtain some satisfaction, but when we are not able to obtain pleasure directly, we try to do something that is socially allowed and through which we can obtain satisfaction, instead of something we desire but which is forbidden to us. Freud called this psychic process sublimation, in which reality is modified to obtain in it what was denied. Creativity is one of the functions of the human capacity for sublimation and sublimation can then be the renunciation of an impossible satisfaction, replaced by plausible and interesting activities for society and culture.

Creativity, as an obligatory process, is shown in the activity of playing, through which a third shared reality is created. Creativity is not just the creation of works of art, but according to Winnicott (2000), it is a given inherent to the fact of living. Baby and toddler become capable of playing with creative activity par excellence. When this individual becomes an adult, this subject replaces the creative capacity of playing with others such as art, science, and even religion.

For Winnicott, playful and artistic activity, a transitional reality as the author says, is not just a defence against the repression of human drives, but support for a psychic balance. The transitional reality always moves the subject to a future where objects and modes of satisfaction, always new, occupy the spaces of the constitutive lack of the human being, which constitutes us as subjects when a third element enters the relationship between mother and baby.

This cut is what allows us to seek other relationships and other substitutive objects to try to obtain satisfaction or pleasure. Psychoanalysis calls this process castration.

Creativity gives rise to an "illusory" reality or transitional reality that is neither the alienation of the subject in his fantasy nor the alienation of the other. The subject can continue his or her existence in this transitional space: where material and memory, repetition and innovation, and also what is provisional and permanent are interconnected.

Winnicott (1975) draws attention to the importance of playing in the child's psychic structuring since it is constituted in the relationship with the mother, with the other, with the world. It is in playing that the child is constituting and discovering himself as a subject. The child has the pleasure of working out his anxieties and acquires experience in playing. Through play, it creates an environment where she can invent, explore and solve problems.

Like playing, cultural experience takes place in a privileged area of human experience, as it is described by a terrain of indeterminate boundaries that make up our reality. It is the place of potential separation between the external world and the internal world, between objective reality and subjective reality. This is what the author says:

"It is here that the use of symbols develops and that they represent, at one and

the same time, the phenomena ofthe external world and the phenomena of the

individualperson being examined. [...] the separation is avoided byfilling the

potentialspacewith creative play, with the use of symbols and with everything

that ends upadding toculturallife." (Winnicott, 1975, p.151)

"In childhood, this intermediate area is necessary for the beginning of a relationship between the child

and the world is made possible by a good enough mothering in the critical primitive phase. Essential

to all this is the continuity (in time) of the external emotional environment and of specific elements in

the physical environment, such as the transitional object or objects." (Winnicott, 1975, p.29)

To talk about the transitional object, Lacan, in the Seminar on Object Relation and Freudian Structures, refers to the toy, analysing the concept developed by Winnicott. According to him; *"[...] even in the youngest child, we see these objects appear that Winnicott calls transitional objects because we cannot say on which side they are situated in the reduced and incarnated dialectic of hallucination and the real object. All objects in a child's games are transitional objects. Toys, strictly speaking, the child does not need to be given, since he creates them from everything he gets his hands on. They are transitional objects. Regarding these, it is not necessary to ask whether they are more subjective or more objective - they are of a different nature. Even if Mr. Winnicott does not go beyond the limits of calling them that, we will simply call them imaginary.*"(Lacan, 1995, p.34)

Lacan does not speak specifically of transitional objects, he uses the concept of imaginary objects to draw a parallel with the connection that Winnicott makes between playing and the intermediate area of human experience. This is the area of transition between reality and imagination, playing occupies this transition space. Through playing, the child tries to give meaning to what is around him, to what is real. The real, the symbolic reminder that escapes the human being, is not the same as the reality that can be symbolized. And it is exactly this reality of the child that the theories of Psychology and Pedagogy cannot grasp.

Mrech (2002) explains that psychology and developmental theories talk about the child through language constructions that were made to talk about them. This confuses the meanings elaborated by the language, as being the child's own thinking. However, it is not possible to express everything in words. There is something that cannot be said. As the author explains: For Lacan, it is important that we realize that there is always something in language and speech that leaks out, something that is not reached, except approximately: the child himself at play. It is in this region that Lacan points out the existence of the register of the real. Something that we try to grasp, but we only identify through the symbols, images, meanings, and meanings of our culture (Mrech, 2002, p.119)

We can only constitute ourselves as subjects and give meaning to the world in relation to the other, to culture, precisely because the first image that the child has of himself comes from the other, whose primary representative is, in general, the mother. According to Levin (1997), it is this look of desire, which the other (maternal) transfers to the child, which will not allow him to reflect on his muscular, tonic, or functional development, but in a place impossible to touch, an invisible place, which lacks tangible (touchable) and visual reality. This place, this hole, without direct relation to the three psychics formulated by the French psychoanalyst Jacques Lacan (1998): the real, the imaginary, and the symbolic. These are the three psychic registers through which Lacan (1998), during the development of his work, tries to account for the human psyche. The three registers intertwine forming a name, called Borromean, a concept of topology, used by Lacan. Imagine a rope, now tie three knots in it, the three registers represent these three knots, if one of them gets out of place, the others also come out and become unbalanced, so the others will not remain connected to each other. It is important to remember that none of the elements work in isolation, they must always be connected. This idea of the rope was precisely for you to understand the meaning of the text.

The psychic record of the Real must not be confused with the common notion of reality. For Lacan, the Real is what remains as the remainder of the Imaginary and the Symbolic, not captured by these two registers. The Real is the impossible, that which cannot be symbolized and remains impenetrable to the subject of desire, for whom reality has a phantasmic nature. Real is what is lacking in the symbolic order, what can only be approximated, never captured. Lacan stated that, in order to be the speaker, there is no exact correspondence for the object and its image, between the parts of the body and the image one has of it. Symbolic refers to the place of the fundamental code of the language. It is law, a regulated structure without which there would be no culture, a place where senses and meanings are formed. Lacan named him the great Other. The Other, spelled in capital letters, was adopted to show that the relationship between the subject and the big Other is different from the relationship with the reciprocal other and similar to the imaginary self.

Speller (2002) says that the subject of Psychoanalysis is the subject of the unconscious, the one structured with a language, the subject constituted in the Symbolic, while the ego, the seat of deception, is constituted in the imaginary relationship with the other, the similar. It is through the meanings given by the Imaginary and the Symbolic that we try to account for the Real. For Lacan, the emergence of meaning takes place in the naming, but the Imaginary that will give consistency and anticipate what will be retaken by the signifying processes. According to the author; *"[...] the consistency, I would say, is of the Imaginary order. What has been demonstrated at length throughout human history, and which should inspire us with singular prudence, is that much of consistency, all consistency that has already proved itself, is pure imagination. Here I bring the Imaginary back its weight of meaning. Consistency, for the speaking being, for the speaking being, is what is manufactured and invented."*(Lacan, 1995, p.30)

Levin (1997) states that the symbolic position that the other reflects and refracts in each look, in each gesture, in each loving touch insists and invests the child, not as an organism of a species, but as a subject of its own destiny and singular. In this same line of reasoning, Fernández comments: *"[...] knowledge possesses the Other, and it can only be acquired indirectly, on the contrary, knowledge, which is a personal construction and grants the possibility of use, is related with incarnating knowledge according to personal characters."*(Fernández, 1990, p.165)

In the play, the child can link ideas with bodily function. According to Winnicott (1982), the game is a doing and for that, the child will need some time from psychomotor doing that will allow him to know how to do with his own body. According to Levin (1997, p.152), in the playful domain of being and having, the child transforms the habits of life into a game. They are like games that later become habits. The child creates and constitutes himself through his creations, his play, he invents by playing or plays by inventing. The child who cannot make sense of play is perhaps because he has not found ways to make sense of his own inner reality. It is precisely in the so-called transitional phenomena, conceptualized by Winnicott (1975), that playing can help, mediating the child with the external world, enabling him to give meaning to what he experiences.

Playing facilitates the apprehension of the external world because, through the playful activity, the child can form concepts, select ideas, make logical relationships, and integrate perceptions. She plays, imitates, and represents through playing. Acting on objects, it structures its space and time. Playing is an important axis in children's education, even because playing, dreaming, and fantasizing, as well as studying, learning, and working, are not independent things, they are psychically intertwined, some influencing each other. All the psychic importance of playing should be considered in the teaching-learning process. Playing helps to solve problems and difficulties, stimulating the creativity and autonomy of the child who is inserted in the symbolic world, in language. Playing also supports the approach of other individuals.

Unlike what the modernity of the present day shows us, which proposes fiction and games only as hobbies and children's entertainment (such as the use of electronics and television), the present work offers a possibility of innovation in the proposal, where playing is conceptualized in another way, as psychoanalytic theories tell us. Kupfer (1998) said that: When an educator works at the service of a subject, he abandons training and adaptation techniques, renounces excessive concern with teaching methods and with strict, absolute, closed, and unquestionable content, as already stated in the conclusion of Freud and education. On the contrary, he only puts the objects of the world at the service of a student; a subject who, anxious to make himself said, anxious to make himself represented in the words and objects of culture, will choose in this offer those that concern him, in which he is implied by his kinship with the first significant inscriptions that gave him form and place in the world.

The teacher can recreate the path of knowledge construction in an original way, with each student, because for each of them, this process will imply unique marks. This can, in fact, give rise to the child's unique subjectivity, trying to apprehend their unique way of being in the world, what happens to them, inferring from evidence brought by the child during play. The teacher can put himself in the place of sustaining his student's desire, in the way of building knowledge.

According to Cunha (2001), playing does not imply a commitment or planning, it mainly involves spontaneous and pleasure-generating behaviours. Play can be transmitted to the child through their own family members, in an expressive way and from generation to generation, or it can be discovered by the child autonomously, outside the family environment, inserted in their social relationships with other children and even within the school environment. In other words, children can experience play spontaneously or not, they can have rules or not, they can play based on their imagination and creation and also based on pre-established rules by the adult.

The toy also provides and encourages free play and fantasy. The child places in the object he is playing with the meaning he wants at the moment. Finally, in the rush of everyday life, parents and teachers often try to simplify their tasks and routines, offering ready-made toys that do not require assembly. Thus, the child develops in an environment far from the ludic, treated as a miniature, within a perspective that the most important thing is to study, learn, acquire knowledge, develop skills, stimulate intelligence, aiming at their preparation for a competitive world. In *"Beyond the Pleasure Principle, Freud (1920)"*deals with the importance of play for the human psyche, he refers to children's play as working methods employed by the mental psychic apparatus in one of its first normal activities. In another article, Creative Writers and Daydreams (1908), Freud addresses play as a child's most intense favourite activity. By playing, she creates a world of her own, readjusting it in a new way that makes sense to her.

Freud (1920) describes the game of a one-and-a-half-year-old child, which he names in German Fort-da. *"Fort"*means to go, and *"da"*means to return. It was the mother's disappearing and returning game, which consisted of a game of reel away making him disappear, and then pulling him back with a happy expression of relief. According to Freud (1920), the play had an obvious relationship with the separation from the mother, a distressing experience that can be elaborated by the child through play and play, which led to support the maternal absence. When the mother leaves the child, when the separation takes place, it is precisely the starting point of the beginning of her experience with play.

The child plays with small objects that he throws away, and with his image in the mirror. According to Meira (2003), in this game, the child can acquire control over absence and presence, as it is he who produces the scene of making himself disappear and appear in front of the mirror, the scene that reveals the constitution of the subject, analysed by Lacan in the writing The mirror stage and its function as a trainer of the self. As Meira says:

-"We have, then, some points that are crucial with regard to the constitution of children's play.

The metaphorisation process, repetition, language, the mirror image, and the real pit were,

there, the mother let the child go. And the small objects with which the child plays: toys."

(Meira, 2003, p.41-3)

According to Freud (1920), this constitutes proof that there are sufficient ways and means to turn what is unpleasant in itself into a theme to be remembered and worked through in the mind. Thus, *"the child, after all, was only able to repeat his unpleasant experience in play because the repetition brought with it the production of pleasure and of another type, a more direct production."* (p.27). Freud also observes that it is an effort by the child to establish the passage from passivity to activity, an inversion that can provide another mode of pleasure, the mastery of a remarkable event, but still relates this last displeasure of the mother's absence, to the point to sustain their production in play.

Playing also underlies the differentiation of an outside and an inside, its exteriority and its own body. The traumatic experience that is put on the scene is the absence of the mother and the mechanism in action is the transformation of this absence into its opposite, which has the function of allowing the passage of the active-passive. From then on, the child who becomes an active agent no longer passively suffers the so-called symbolic or necessary violence, an important point that can be directly related to playing.

Kupfer (2001) highlights the importance of Piera Aulagnier when she develops this theoretical concept called symbolic violence. Aulagnier emphasizes, first, that a mother attributes meanings to everything that, initially, is nothing more than the pure reflex action of a piece of meat. This attribution of meanings is accompanied by the assumption that there is already a subject responsible for cutting and moulding a subject on that piece of meat. Thus, there was an encounter with the Other, which meant something to the child who gave him a name.

According to Kupfer (2001), from this formulation, it is deduced that there is an imposition of the Symbolic, of language, on the body: the idea of founding interpretive violence. When, by culture, a word is imposed on some movement experienced by a baby, all other expressive possibilities disappear, to speak of this unique experience of a unique subject. As he says, it's as if the mother said: *"What you're feeling is called that, and it's not talked about anymore."* (p.141). The subject is forced to renounce his unique and irreparable sensation that exists because it is nameable, recognizable in a world shared by a common code.

For the child to be able to elaborate this violence, giving it meaning, their fictions are necessary in the imaginary and creative world of play, which connects the subjective to the objective. It is in the intermediate zone of creation, and in its transit, that the child articulates the senses for its existence when experiencing the world. That is, when we talk about violence in Education, we do not refer to violent parents who like to beat their children, but to the necessarily violent character that exists in the establishment of the Law that is given in castration, that is, what Lacan calls the paternal function: the cut that is made in the dual relationship between mother and child, the entry of a third element so that the child can constitute himself as a subject in the world of language, of culture.

"The violence of Education, inevitable and structuring, is called symbolic violence that presents itself

to the subject at every moment, at every step, in every learning situation, at everyconfrontation with

the limit, as not, with the death."(Kupfer, 2001, p.142)

We see, then, in the fortda case, an example of how play, like humour, promotes emptying of meaning, and how making it appear or disappear becomes a space for new possibilities of meaning. Regarding humour, Freud (1928) states that, like jokes and the comic, humour has something liberating, but it also has something great and elevated, which the other two ways mentioned, of obtaining pleasure through intellectual activity, lack. He explains about the Ego's refusal (Chapter 6) to be afflicted by the provocations of reality, affected by the traumas of the external world. Humour actually demonstrates, according to Freud, that these traumas from the external world are nothing more than opportunities for pleasure: *"Humour is not resigned, but rebellious. It means not only the triumph of the ego, but also of the pleasure principle, which can assert itself against the cruelty of real circumstances."*(Freud, 1928, p.166). This possibility of escaping suffering through humour highlights one of the many methods that the human mind builds to get rid of the compulsion to suffer. The human being lives in a constant struggle between the death drive and the life drive. In this respect, adult humour has a function very similar to that of play for children. It can be an attempt to resign a distressing experience, through something that brings pleasure. As Freud says:

"[...] the main one is the intention that the humour conveys, whether acting in relation to the

self or to other people. It means: Look! Here is the world, which looks so dangerous! It is

nothing more than a children's game, worthy only of being a joke!" (1927, p.169)

According to Bogomoletz (1995), in 1927, already talking about the topic of ego, superego, ID, Freud revises and reorganizes his thinking about what is funny, approaching mainly humour, no longer the joke. His interpretation of the fact that humour provokes laughter is: we laugh at what is comical, at what is funny in our eyes, as when we see something that, due to its inadequacy or strange appearance, makes us laugh. Bogomoletz (1995) says that the metapsychology of mood, according to Freud, began with an emphasis on tensions that should be discharged. But Freud observed that it was not just a matter of discharging the negative charges produced by the drives. In fact, difficult situations that needed something in the order of elaboration could be turned into something funny, thus becoming less painful. In this way, humour is something that can be understood as a look capable of laughing and finding some pleasure in everyday difficulties, trying to elaborate on the suffering caused by the demands and pressures of life (in addition to the difficulties inherent in human relationships). As an example, we could call the good-humoured guy who always jokes about life's difficulties, but that doesn't mean he doesn't take life seriously. A good-humoured person tries to live in a more creative way, looking in humour for ways to transform reality into something constructive, less painful and more pleasurable.

We can cite games like poetry and art, where the same game is updated, and in place of the object (The pawn) can be the word. For Winnicott (1975), the child plays dropping objects and emphasizes that the game of retaining and releasing, in addition to establishing the object and its conservation, also institutes the possibility of its lack. It is she who moves desire. Through the lack, the child can create ways to fill this space with other objects and relationships, establishing in play a bridge between desire and what can be achieved in reality. Playing, which for Winnicott is an original doing, approaches the fort-da situation, in which the double movement of finding and creating is fundamental for the subject to be able to recognize the world in its concrete existence and, thus, constitute different possibilities of senses of reality.

According to Freud (1920), play is also influenced by a desire that dominates the child: the desire to grow up and do what adults do. And it doesn't always take a special imitative impulse to provide a reason for play. According to the author, the repetition, the re-experience of something is, in itself, a source of pleasure for the child who does not get tired of asking them to repeat a game that was taught to him, until he is exhausted.

Benjamin (2002) says that it is exactly through our playful rhythms that, for the first time, we become masters of ourselves. Benjamin suggests that studies should be carried out to examine the law that, above all particular rules and rhythms, governs the entirety of the game world: the law of repetition. We know that for the child he is the soul of the game, that nothing makes him happier than once again. Benjamin compares the repetition compulsion present in play with the strong sexual drive in love.

And it was no accident that Freud believed he had discovered something beyond the pleasure principle in this compulsion. And, in fact, each and every deeper experience insatiably desires, until the end of all things, repetition and return, re-establishment of the primordial situation from which it took the initial impulse (Benjamin, 2002, p.101). The child re-creates himself, the whole lived fact. In playing, he tries to work out difficult facts and anguish, but he also experiences, again and more intensely, success and victories. Comparing narrating with playing, Benjamin ponders: When an adult narrates an experience, he relieves his heart of horrors, he enjoys doubly happiness. The child re-creates the full-lived fact for himself, that is, he starts again from the beginning. [...] The essence of playing is not an *"always doing it again"*, but an *"always doing it a new one"*, transforming the experience into a habit. For it is playing, and nothing else, that gives birth to habit. Eating, sleeping, dressing, washing should be instilled in the restless little one playfully, with the accompaniment of the rhythm of verses. Habit enters life as a game, and in it, even in its most rigid forms, it survives until the end of a little game (Benjamin, 2002, p.101-102).

Children's stories, which children enjoy so much, increasingly give way to images. Today, everything that is said must be illustrated, recorded. Corso (2006) considers everything that made the glory of a good storyteller - sounds, silences, intonation, and dramatic ability - was being replaced by the narrative abilities of film and television studios and book and illustrators, comics. But of the main changes, the most interesting is that, even so, some of them subsist through these changes and have lasted, evoking the same emotions in children as well as in adults.

In children, it is easier to see the impact that fiction can have. They cling to some story and with that try to elaborate their dramas. What remains of a story, for the child, is what resonates in their subjectivity. She asks you to tell her stories, often specifying the type of story desired. She wants to play with the characters in the story and pretends to be them, an example is in the comic book by Monica's gang, where the title is Against in against fairies. In this comic, parents tell classic stories but Against plays with the characters, changing the course of the story to something more compared to today's reality. Corso (2006, p.29) states that these exchanges between the adult and the child, with the stories as intermediaries, can operate with a kind of unconscious dialogue. She talks about the fascination of tales in the relationships of adults with children. She also claims that there is a meeting, between fairy tales and children, that rarely fails. In stories told by an adult narrator, or through books, TV, school, cinema, theatre, every child can find sources of fantasy and fiction to support reality.

Freud (1908), in the article Creative Writers and Daydreams, talks about play as the child's favourite and most intense activity. When playing, the child creates a world of his own, readjusts the elements of his world in a new way that has more meaning for him. The child begins to take play seriously and spends a lot of investment on it. As Freud says, *"the antithesis of playing is not what is serious, but what is real."*(Freud, 1908, p.135) Thus, Freud brings the idea that the child perfectly distinguishes his play from reality, but likes to make connections between objects, imaginary situations and visible things in the real world. What Freud says about play and reality is important. Freud says the following:

"When the child grows up and stops playing, after struggling for a few decades to take the realities of life with due seriousness,

he may one day find himself in a mental situation in which this opposition between play and reality disappears once again. As an

adult, he can reflect on the intense seriousness with which he played his games in childhood, equating his present occupations,

apparently so serious, with his childhood games, he can free himself from the heavy burden imposed by life and conquerintense

pleasure if provides by humour." (Freud, 1908, p.136)

The child's play, according to Freud (1908), is largely determined by desires, more precisely by a single desire that helps in the structuring of their psyche: the desire to be big and adult. As adults, we often mourn the loss of our ability to deal with life in a more spontaneous, light-hearted, playful way. Through play, the child represents elements of the external world and internalizes them, building their own way of thinking. Winnicott (1975) states that playing, as a child's experience, is always creative, continuity of space, time is a basic way of living. He says: "Playing is the evident and constant proof of the creative capacity, which means experience." (Winnicott, 1982, p.163) Reinforcing the author's ideas, Levin (1997, p.152) says: "*Childhood cannot be conceived without the playful dimension that aligns and intertwines representations with things. There is no connection or learning in development without this virtual mirror that playful production implies.*"

It is in play that the child connects ideas and bodily function. There cannot be a construction of knowledge if one does not play with knowledge. When talking about play, reference is not made to an act or a product, but to a process. I refer again to this place and time, which Winnicott (1975) calls a transitional space of trust, of creativity. The transition between believing and not believing, inside and outside, the impossible and the necessary of children's tales, of games.

Here I try to address some points that link playing with the issue of creativity at school. Think of the baby who is born and who does not yet discriminate the world, who feels a discomfort whose need manifests with the comfort of being with the mother, at the right time and place. This experience creates for the baby, which we can also call a new being, an illusion of omnipotence because he feels that he created the world from his needs. It is the origin of creativity and belief in the world itself.

Creativity is part of discovering yourself and the world around you. It is in the potential space, discussed by Winnicott (1975), that creation is present through play, that it has the possibility of constituting itself as a subject and as an active subject that can create and take care of the world around it. The following quote touches precisely on the question of the potential space of play and creativity based on life experience: *"The special characteristic of this place in which play and cultural experience have a position is that it depends, for its existence, on experiences of living, not inherited tendencies. A baby is sensitively treated at the time when the mother is separating from him, so the play area is immense; another baby has such an unhappy experience at this stage of his development that it gives him little opportunity to develop, except in terms of introversion or extroversion."*(Winnicott, 1975, p.150)

Based on this concept and these considerations, the teacher can facilitate the creative and non-submissive interaction of the subject with the world. It can also present the student with historically accumulated knowledge, considered relevant by the school, at the appropriate time and in the appropriate way. The teacher could be concerned with receiving the student in a sensitive way, especially at the beginning of the schooling process and in other critical stages, in order to get to know him better to facilitate his transition to the school culture. When we talk about transition, passing, and not adaptation, submission, and adjustment, it is necessary to know who each student is. And then come those basic questions: Where did you come from? What is your rhythm, your style, your beliefs, your values, your habits, your needs, and your conceptions? What do you already know? How did you build your knowledge? How do you use it? Where and how will you use school culture? You can observe students in their singularities, but not judge them by appearance (Stereotype, chapter one, Prejudice, and Perception) Try to invest in the potential space between the subject and the external world in the process, in the passage listening to the students. By listening to the student, more than getting to know him better, the teacher allows him to listen to himself, to be surprised by thinking, doing, being. Facilitating and promoting varied forms of expression, rescuing school history, asking questions, recognizing and valuing what has already been constituted by the student, and identifying the values and references of their group of origin, would be basic functions of the teacher concerned with the human subject.

According to Winnicott (1975), the teacher could explore the potential space between him and his student, being open to listen and establish an exchange relationship, presenting information for which the student is ready to recreate. The relationship of knowledge created and found should be considered in the teaching-learning process, so that the student could appropriate relevant content in a unique and creative way, according to their conceptions and needs. It is essential that they experience school contents, initially, as objects of their own experience, facilitating the transition between the culture of the country where they live and the school culture. The teacher must facilitate the process, helping the student to constitute transitional objects as objects of culture, that is, their social insertion. Safra (1994) talks about the role of the analyst, which we can also trace a similarity in the parallel role of the teacher. Safra says that being open to listening and allowing reflections and associations is a requirement of the analyst. The teacher could also move in this direction with his students, accomplishing something significant. Each teacher, stripped of prejudices, would find a particular way of getting to know their students and providing them with opportunities to express themselves and show their own needs. The teacher, when reading this text, can imagine that he is unaware of reality, a classroom full of students, an extensive program to be explored, bureaucratic tasks to be performed, low salaries, little professional recognition, in relation to some teachers surveyed. We live in a social reality where the educational system makes this movement of the teacher difficult.

However, this approximation in relation to the student's reality, especially at the beginning of the schooling process, is possible and desirable.

For better reflection, I remind you when we talked in the previous paragraphs of this chapter about the mother's role as a mirror that reflects the baby's face, allowing him to feel like a real person, in a satisfying real world and more effective with her participation. For Winnicott (1975), the mother can express to the baby what he is and what he can and has, not just what he would like him to be. The mother's adaptation to the baby's being is what establishes her ability to create, to perceive the external world, and not just adapt to it. Looking at the student and recognizing what he is, what he can, and what he has already built, is the first step that the school can take towards helping the growth and enrichment of every child, and also of the community. For this to occur, the teacher also needs to be recognized in his or her uniqueness, bearing personal characteristics and styles. To respect, the teacher must be respected; he must have his needs and values covered by the educational policy and be socially valued.

In current education and from the psychoanalytic perspective, there is also what could be called creative or citizen education. The introduction of a look, a new way of seeing ourselves and others, of learning to live with differences and changes. The important thing is not to get stuck only in the imaginary, because playing would have an essentially symbolic function: it helps to transform reality and create new ways of being in the world.

PSYCHOANALYSIS AND ITS RELATIONS WITH EDUCATION

Psychoanalysis is defined as a field that deals with the repressed representations of the subject that, although unconscious, can return to the form of dreams, faulty acts, or other unconscious formations. Psychoanalysis has the unconscious as its object of study, one of the most important characteristics that differentiate it from other schools, including Psychology. Speller (2004) says that the other schools, despite variations in object and method, define the study of human behaviour as a field of Psychology, excluding the dimension of a psychic activity that escapes consciousness. The same author (2003) asks: How to engage Psychoanalysis contemporaneously beyond the clinic? How has Psychoanalysis accompanied the changes in subjectivity in the current world? The answers are not easy, however, it is significant to try to answer these questions. It is believed that Psychoanalysis can help everyone who thinks about the unease in culture, as it theorizes about the human and its relations with the world and with people.

For Psychoanalysis, Education is defined as social discourse, implying transmission of culture. In this way, "the intersections between Psychoanalysis and Education occur in a broader field than Psychoanalysis through culture understood as a discursive flow, oral or written." (Calligaris, 1997, p.194) The subject of the unconscious, according to Psychoanalysis, is constituted by language. Thus, to show the possibilities of this field of knowledge with Education, we have to listen to the social discourse, that is, to listen to our objective of this book, what teachers have to say. According to Kupfer (2001, p.118);

"[...] by recognizing Education as social discourse, Psychoanalysis starts to dialogue with it in schools, in the media, in the university".

For the author, an articulation of Psychoanalysis with the social discourse by Education is also understood as social discourse, thus

expanding a lot of meaning. Both the work of the psychoanalyst and the educator, thus aiming to emphasize the author. "[...] expands

the psychoanalyst's field of action, which includes a school institution as a place of listening. The educator will also see himself, in his

turn,led to lead his action in another direction; at the very least, he will stop making so many referrals to psychologists and, at themost,

he will take responsibility for his educational acts."(Kupfer, 2001, p.34)

From this perspective, educating for the author and for other psychoanalysts "becomes the discursive social practice responsible for the child's immersion in the language, making them capable, in turn, of producing the discourse, that is, of addressing the other making a social bond with it." (Kupfer, 2001, p.35) As Speller (2004) explains, little has been explored about the contributions of Psychoanalysis to Education, because, traditionally, it has been seen as a field of clinical application only. What has been expected since then from a psychoanalytically oriented work at school is the opening of a space for speeches, making everyone's words circulate, without a master who holds the absolute truth, because teachers need to question and seek answers that imply directly into your doing.

There is an opinion about playing as a waste of time. Perhaps this is a reflection of the thinking of modernity and its discourse in which the relationship with time is one of productivity, the do "Time is Money" (it is time for money), in which the human being from childhood is pressured to produce, make money and be successful. In this line of thinking, teachers say that playing at school does not provide income, it disperses the child, and parents demand tasks and full notebooks for their children because children must produce and learn. In this way, what is excellent for parents and teachers is that the child has a lot of work and doesn't waste time with anything else. Playing is something that should be done outside of school, and even then, with some restrictions.

Nowadays, children are much busier, they have to study, learn to compute, do various sports, practice languages and others: All this with excellence. Even though these are not a requirement for a child of low social class, such as those who live in the periphery, to study in public schools, the social discourse refers to the idea that one must produce and consume to be someone in life. Children are affected by this type of demand, both by teachers and parents. In this way, the demand for learning takes on great weight and free time, time to play, is not seen as something positive and necessary.

Today, children are making ever-increasing demands on toys and programs. It's just that, like adults, they have [

valued the end more than the means. And the taste of doing anything or doing nothing in the companywe like

has been lost (Sayao, 2000, p.182).

This bombardment of stimuli, contrary to what many think, can lead children to a lack of desire, because, as Psychoanalysis claims, desire needs lack desire. As Speller (2004, p. 61) says: "*Although important, it is not the availability of information that will make the child want to learn.*" Modernity demands that everything be done quickly and efficiently, and the child is present in the midst of a lot of activities. Even the child who studies in the public school in the periphery is subject to charges, as they are also immersed in social discourse. So, the question remains: when will the child create his fiction, his toys, his fantasies, his stories, his adventures? Is it possible for a child to live without it? Is it possible for a child to learn without creating? Is it possible to humanize oneself without playing? In my opinion, no. Because through playing, stories, creations, we learn to be in the world, making connections with the subjective world and the various realities with which we live.

Levin (200) says that a child is only the act he produces, making his production a mirror that allows him, on the one hand, to recognize himself and, on the other hand, to ignore himself. It is to this lack of knowledge and uncertainty that the child surrenders more easily than the adult.

METHODOLOGY

The methodology is a word derived from "method", from the Latin "methodus" whose meaning is "path or way to accomplish something". A method is a process of achieving a certain end or arriving at knowledge. The methodology is the field in which the best methods practised in a given area for the production of knowledge are studied. The methodology consists of a meditation on logical and scientific methods. Initially, the methodology was described as an integral part of the logic that focused on the different modalities of thought and application. Subsequently, the notion that the methodology told us was something exclusive to the field of logic that was abandoned over time, as the methods were applied in various areas of knowledge. Today the methodology for each area serves differently, but they all concern organization, administration, services, tips for a good job, and a lot of practice. Each area has its own methodology. The teaching methodology is the application of different methods in the teaching-learning process. The main teaching methods used in Brazil are Traditional Method, Constructivism, Social Interactionism, and Montessori Method. A research methodology may vary according to its nature. Thus, research can present quantitative, qualitative, basic, or applied characteristics. Scientific methodology It is the discipline that deals with the scientific method. It is the structure of the different sciences and is based on the systematic analysis of phenomena and the organization of rational and experimental principles and processes. It allows, through scientific investigation, the acquisition of scientific knowledge. Teaching methodology The teaching methodology is an expression that has tended to replace the expression "didactic", which has gained a pejorative connotation because of the formal and abstract character of its schemes that are not well inserted in true pedagogical action. Thus, the teaching methodology is the part of pedagogy that is directly concerned with the organization of student learning and its control. Methodology and Final Paper. The methodology of scientific work, for example, for the completion of a course conclusion work (commonly called FP), is the part in which a detailed and rigorous description of the object of study and the techniques used in the research activities is made.

QUALITATIVE RESEARCH IN EDUCATION AND PSYCHOANALYSIS

The present research adopts a qualitative methodology which, according to Luke (1986), is quite flexible and presents a socializing character, in addition to seeking to carry out a synthesis regarding the involvement of the researcher and the researched group. The qualitative approach in Education tries to bring research closer to the educator's daily life. The knowledge acquired is always marked by the signs of its time, committed to historical reality and not to absolute truth. Qualitative research can be understood as a possibility of transforming the way of thinking and researching in Social Sciences. Thus, with the rigour of scientific work, qualitative research also focuses on the participation of the researcher and the group being worked on, instead of questionnaires or correlation coefficients, typical of experimental analyses. Qualitative research brings the researcher much closer to reality. Through intense fieldwork, according to Luke and Andrew (1986), qualitative research proposes a direct and prolonged contact of the researcher with the environment and the situation being investigated. An important factor of this approach is that the people, the gestures, the words studied must always be related to the context in which they appear. The data collected is predominantly analytical.

Some quotes are also used to support a statement or to clarify a certain point of view. All the data that appear in this context of the reality studied are important. Thus, the researcher can focus his attention on as many elements as possible present in the situation. In the qualitative approach, according to Babier (2002), the concern with the process is much greater than with the product. We have to know how to listen more and not get carried away only by appearances (for reflection, go back to chapters one and two), as researchers in Education. One of several types of qualitative research is action research, which has some of its most significant characteristics. According to Luke (1986), it is conceived and carried out in close association with the action or resolution of a collective problem, with which researchers and participants are involved in a cooperative or participatory way. The knowledge about the researched fact is built from the question that the researcher asks the collected data and based on everything he knows about the subject, in addition to the accumulated theories about it.

In action research, according to Babier (2002), the production of knowledge is also done by the participants of the research that is done with others and not only about the other. The other is not used only as an object of study, as this type of investigation also affects us as researchers. Qualitative research, in the conception of action research, for example, works as a facilitator, so that the people involved can delineate the central problems. In the case of Children's Education, the work with teachers, taking as a reference the scope of playing at school, had as a point of origin, for the group discussions, the difficulties that they themselves had in including this play in their professional practice.

At the beginning of the study, there are very broad focuses of interest that, in the end, become more direct and specific. The qualitative study involving the collection of analytical data, obtained from the researcher's direct contact with what is being studied, emphasizes, even more, the process than the final product, prioritizing portraying the perspective of educators. According to Psychoanalysis, the adopted reference, the researcher's listening to Education professionals is a key point, in order to promote some changes so that something new emerges. This would be one of the greatest contributions of Psychoanalysis to Education. It directs us to a listening that is beyond discourse, what is called floating listening. Babier (2002) says that this listening would be like listening to an empty place, that is, it provides a creative void, with no place for the researcher's interpretation, but rather, for the individual himself to be involved in what he says.

The researcher tries to focus on information that includes preconceptions and prejudgements to listen to the other. These are other approaches that are more concerned with an explanation of a given fact, an interpretation that offers little space for the subject and, therefore, for the possibilities of change. It is important to give voice to the subject so that he can be involved in the research process, taking responsibility for his speeches and for his own actions. As Babier (2002) says, this listening has the critical role of making people participate and change, as they involve themselves in their own work. It can be said that the research group works as training for personal change, where experiences and reflections on their practice can be exchanged. The group has the possibility to work on the issues that arise during the process, in addition to being able to assess the effects resulting from their actions.

THE SCENARIO AND SUBJECTS OF THE RESEARCH

The school chosen for the research was the Municipal School of Basic Education / EMEB Liberdade, located in the Osmar Cabral neighborhood in Cuiabá-MT. The interest in developing the study at this school arose from a contact between a supervisor and other teachers who explained how Escola Liberdade differs from most schools for children's education, as it has a pedagogical proposal for teaching through play, emerging an immediate relationship with the theme of this book. The creation of this school was due to the need to serve some children considered surplus in the municipal education network. The Secretary of Education, however, wanted a different proposal for the new school, whose project had as one of its pedagogical lines to work with playing to teach.

THE PATH WALKED AND THE OBTAINING OF RESULTS AND CATEGORIES

Seven weekly meetings were held at the EMEB school. The discussion categories defined based on common and most significant elements that appear in the teachers' speeches were: learning by playing in the conception of a new project; aggressive play and its limits; play and reality.

- **The first category;**learning while playing in the conception of a new project, synthesizes the teachers' concern in developing the school's proposal of working with playing to learn, their difficulties in fulfilling the proposed project and the notion of how far playing is far from the reality of the school.

- **The second category;**aggressive play and its limits, mainly deal with the issue of aggression and violence in the context of playing and school, in addition to addressing the issue of teacher authority and the difficulty he has in establishing limits for play.

- **The third category;**play and reality, present how teachers think they can teach children something about reality.

Is this possible without playing? In this third category, I present the material that was collected from more than one hundred students by psychology students at FUMT. First, they collected the material and read two questions that were important to the chapter in this book:

What is play for you?

Do you think the adult plays?
Why do you think children play?

Thus, everyone responded differently and clearly in writing. After the studies, before doubts and discussions about what had been presented, they shared information and asked us to ask the same questions again. So there were some notes about the day of class.

DISCUSSION ABOUT THE CATEGORIES

Learning by playing in a new conception

The proposal of the school, where the research was carried out, is based on a new idea: Teaching while playing is a project that brings playfulness with central importance to early childhood education. This results, in the teachers' speeches, a great concern to develop this work well, seen as a great challenge that worries for the difficulty and, at the same time, attractive for the novelty. It is not easy to work with a new proposal. Even with classroom experience, teachers feel like beginners, as if they have never worked with children. They almost always think that children are the same, that everyone, in the same age group, should learn in the same way.

The teachers have in their hands a new project that was presented to them without a prior discussion about what they thought of it, and without their having participated in its elaboration. Some talk about the difficulty of understanding the project and how to use play to teach, mainly because they do not believe that playing can work as a pedagogical tool. They think that playing is to discharge energy. Even those who agree with the proposal offered by the school also find it difficult to execute the project.

During the meetings, the teachers made exactly these associations: playing is only during recess and during the teachers' coffee break. This idea is also very prevalent in daycare centres. Teachers usually say they are frustrated with their school practice, as they invest a lot in the programming of classes and the children do not correspond to the results idealized by them in the project. They put as ideal goals the reason to learn and not play. As students do not act in a comprehensive way, teachers feel very discouraged, and this happens perhaps because they still seem to be very connected to the homogenizing discourse of Pedagogy and Psychology: children in the same age group must have the same developmental processes as their peer's same patterns of answers for the class to pass because some students learn and others don't, and so they agree that the same should be for all students.

In order for children to look at it in a different and understanding way, teachers must take a different look, that is, Levin (1997) says that there is no development equal to the other. In subjective structuring, there is no chronological time. What operates is the logical time of the world of the signifier. According to the author; [...] The time of the subjective structure belongs to the discursive dimension. Although the significant elements conform to the subject's structure, the subject's encounter with different events in a diachrony marks the indeterminacy of this encounter and the intertwining effects that such acts produce in the structure itself (Levin, 1997, p.24). Teachers follow norms, rules, and recipes to avoid human vicissitudes in dealing with life, they usually do not take a look at the specifics of each child, with labels occurring within each categorization (chapter one), in this way:

"The good guy can never be aggressive, the smart guy is not seen and accepted when he doesn't know.

The child misses the opportunity to discover who he really is, and to feel accepted as such. [...]Creation

takes place when, at the moment of the spontaneous gesture, in which the child is ready to create, there is an environment that meets it, giving it an outline that does not take away its originality. Offering a ball to

those who are experimenting with the possibility of kicking, a doll for those who need to feel like theirmother,

aform ofdivision for those who want to know how to equitably distribute the stickers that the group has won,

are opportunitiesfor the potential to transform it into something conquered."(Sanches, 2002, p.37)

The Other is decisive in the constitution of the subject. The Other of the desire that constitutes us, a vestige of the primordial, specific Other that received me in this world. The author says that the subject's desire does not have its origin in the body, but is shaped by what this Other desired for him. She also says, "therefore, the first position of the subject to come is that of object-cause of desire, a position in which the Other's desire has placed him." (Rudge, 1987, p.85) After that, what you want is to cause the Other's desire, to put yourself back in the role of the cause of desire, but the Other's desire is also an enigma, it cannot be unravelled. Rudge (1987) speaks of fantasy as a response that the subject offers to the Other's desire, in order not to have to respond to this desire with his own being an object. The school plays an important role in the child's access to synthesized knowledge, but there is another important role that it must play: helping children to free themselves from their parents, that is, it is about finding new references, different from those that parents have brought, different from those that the child has at home. Sayao (2003) talks about Family Education to which one should be aware: the expectation of parents towards the child. Even if parents are not aware of this, this issue, pointed out by Sayão, is crucial for their children. But it is essential to emphasize that the parents must support the child, teaching ethical values, showing the possible paths, placing the necessary limits so that later they are able to make their own choices. When the child goes to school, he/she finds a space to experience references that are different from those of the family.

Raising children

THE DREAM CHILD AND THE REAL CHILD

As soon as the child is born, the parents must face a decisive challenge: they have to say goodbye to the dreamed child and welcome, accept and adopt the real child, with all its peculiarities, such as physical appearance, gender, and ways of behaving. This will be even more difficult if the child you have in your arms is very different from the one you expected. Unlike the child who cries non-stop, who came into the world bald and red as a tomato, giving the impression of not wanting to accept the world outside the womb, it creates a series of problems. All the fantasies built up by the wonderful pictures of babies in parenting magazines are undone. And maybe it's a girl when the parents prefer a boy, or worse still, the baby was born prematurely, in danger of becoming disabled, and it may be that it is already certain of that.

The small child is what he is. The more you love her, the better she will develop. In the first few months, this means, in practice, is available to the baby at all times. Seek physical contact with affectionate touches and massages, have regular and routine care, feed him, talk to him, hold him in your lap and sleep close to him. Love is really an activity, if you want to go back to talking about feelings within the family, go back to chapter three. However, parents should know that it is exactly this type of behaviour that will be the basis for a secure bond. And a secure connection with the parents is, in the first years of life, the presupposition for all the mental and emotional development of the child.

Even in premature children, development is less problematic if they experience to touch and physical contact. It is interesting that newborns have numerous skills that allow them to take the initiative to get in touch with someone, thus establishing a connection. Intuitively, most parents react to these signals by increasingly tightening the bonds of love. If you can accept your child as he is, if you are able to take care of him reliably and if you give him all the security, snuggling his small body against your big body, then that child will receive a stable base to continue its development like a human being.

Every baby deserves the most love. People who are marked by a positive mother complex naturally feel the right to exist, are creative, and know how to live by letting others live. They know the right to be treated with respect, the right to express the needs of body and soul, to fulfil themselves, and to participate in the goods of life.

Psychologist Verena Kast calls the first relationship with the mother a positive mother complex. Similarly, there is the positive mother complex according to the Jungian theory, a complex arises from an important intention between two people. Surely, you are familiar with the inferiority complex, which arises when a person is systematically belittled by the people in his environment. No person is worth less than the other. But if one hears others say this all the time, he will end up believing it.

People who are marked by a positive mother complex naturally feel the right to exist, are creative, and know how to live by letting others live. They know the right to express the needs of body and soul (chapters two and three), to fulfil themselves, and to participate in the goods of life. They feel charged by life and feel the pleasure of the body, of food, of sexuality, of being alive. Thus, the small child gets to know different types of relationships and learns to have different expectations in front of them. Not depending exclusively on the mother, she will face new situations more easily and will have more options to react. While the little girl sees her mother as a similar being, the fascination of the stranger emanates from her father, which is very important from the beginning. Many winning women had fathers who influenced these independent and autonomous personalities, and who, in the eyes of these women, were attractive, intelligent, ambitious, active and liberal.

SAY YES AND SAY NO

Many adults say no, that is, they deny it a lot. Therefore, we must be aware that it is important to know how to say yes and know how to say no, and also to have the possibility to do so within the family. If we accept each other as personalities, we can make necessary decisions. If your son or daughter, for breakfast, asks for chocolate milk, and you don't have it at home, that means no.

He/she will be disappointed and if he/she is small he/she will start to complain and cry asking for chocolate milk.

- How do you feel when this happens? Do you say to yourself: is it normal to be disappointed, but is it also normal to express disappointment in this way, crying and asking?

- Or do you feel guilty about your child?

- Or do you become aggressive and impatient?

For better reflection, return to chapter one or continue reading. Observe yourself in these situations and understand that it is okay to say no to a child. But often, you also have to say yes, because every yes is important for the child's development. Some children live in a world of prohibitions, which jeopardizes their development and their intelligence: getting dirty in a puddle of water, playing with the mud, climbing trees, messing up the pan cupboard, fiddling with appropriate scissors (without sharps and preferably made of plastic), cooking something on the stove... All this should be allowed for children. Unlike other children, they never lose or have no limits, hence the guidance. If everything is allowed, a child becomes totally insecure and spoiled. Saying no, when, for example, she is in front of the television or wants a certain t-shirt, it doesn't hurt, on the contrary! You can also say no if you feel tired or exhausted and need a break. Explain to the child why you cannot play with them right now and when you will have time to be with them again.

In families where it is permissible to say no, it is also possible to say yes, from the heart. Thus, everyone is at ease, each one can, within their limits, make their own decisions. Be a role model for your child When living with children, you always have to ask yourself: What is important to me? Giving an answer to this question and knowing our values and criteria, thus defining our priorities. And that will have consequences for family life.

Your children judge you by the example you set for them. Whoever smokes one cigarette after another, has no credibility to demand from their children a conscious behaviour in relation to health. And if you, as an adult, play a lot with children, you don't need to give great explanations about the importance of the joy of living. Because children feel it.

Sincerity is a value that adults often demand from children, without setting a good example. Think about how many times you have lied and in which situations you have disproved your convictions. One day, your children will want to talk about it with you. Children are always asking questions, making them reflect on life and our values. This happens because they want to discover the world, they are curious and whenever they hear something new they want to tell us. This is very important! Even if in a conversation you defend an opinion that is completely opposite to your daughter's, she will remember the conversation for a lifetime if you treat her with respect and dignity. And if she contradicts you, it doesn't mean she won't agree with you in the future.

THE FIRST YEARS IN A CHILD'S LIFE

In speech development, most girls are well ahead of boys. While ten-month-old girls already know how to speak three words, boys can only speak one, according to research.

Scientific Facts

At 18 months, half of the girls already have a vocabulary of 56 words, while half of the boys only use 28 words. Differences are confirmed in the passive vocabulary. At 16 months, fifty percent of girls understand 206 words, while the same percentage of boys understand only 134 words. Only at the age of 20 months, many boys are equal to girls. It is an irrefutable fact that girls generally have the greater verbal ability because they activate the left temporal lobe (left side) of the brain earlier, which is the centre of verbal ability. And it's because girls talk more that the brain is stimulated and helps to build connections that are indispensable for the child's future intelligence, creativity, and adaptability. The speech acquisition phase is marked by alternating effects that, over the years, appear even more clearly. If there are conditions to provide bilingual education to your children, in the case, for example, of mother and father not speaking the same native language, the opportunity should not be missed. Never again will a child learn a language as easily and spontaneously as in the first years of life. In addition, learning a second language will mostly have positive effects on a child's intelligence.

Multiple kinds of research show that in kindergartens, educators treat girls and boys differently. Often, girls' verbal efforts are supported, thus encouraging their natural talent in the field. In general, parents give the necessary stimuli spontaneously. Starting to talk to the baby, explaining what they are doing with him, singing to him, or later reading stories. If these stimuli are not given, the child's development will be retarded and even stop, as happens, for example, with children of deaf-mutes, if there is no other person to assume the role that would be the parents.

In the United States, a thirteen-year-old girl was released from captivity where her parents had kept her imprisoned like an animal. Even after getting the best possible care in another environment, she never learned to speak properly. And who hasn't heard of Kaspar Hauser, an abandoned boy of unknown origin who appeared in 1828, as an adult, in Nuremberg located in Germany, had a developmental disorder, by the psychology of the 20th century. In previous chapters we talked about eating disorders and mental disorders, maybe this can help you.

WHAT DO SPORTS, MUSIC, AND CLAY HAVE TO DO WITH INTELLIGENCE?

A newborn child has approximately 100 billion nerve cells. Only a small part of them are connected according to a genetically determined scheme. The rest is up to learning. With perception through the senses and with motor processes, bundles are formed in the nervous system that allows the child to learn and automate movements. In babies, we can very well observe how this happens.

Scientific Facts

Around three months of age, a baby begins to observe his own hands and learns to bring them to his mouth. The eyes, mouth, and hands are the parts of the body that, through perception and motor processes, allow the first targeted movements. The repetition of a movement often forms a bundle in the nervous system, the contact between the involved nerves is released, and the movement is performed later automatically. In the fifth month, the baby learns to pick up objects. Sensations emanating from an object are transmitted through nerve cells and electrical impulses directly to the brain. In the opposite direction, impulses are sent from the brain to the muscles, which allows for targeted movements. Feeling and looking at an object, the child distinguishes various meanings of words such as ball, mother, car. A small child always learns from sensory perception. And this can be seen from the birth of the child to the infant stage.

If the child plays an instrument like the piano, his brain plays a role in activating all parts of the brain. Music, sport, drawing, plastic arts are not simply pleasurable activities, but also stimulate intelligence in general, as long as the child engages in them voluntarily and not by force.

The farewell of nappies

The vast majority of girls get out of nappies early and without problems, except for boys. To encourage your child to give up nappies, start by taking your child to the bathroom with you if he or she expresses interest. If your child doesn't want to go to the bathroom with you, then be patient. If the child expresses interest, take him to the bathroom and ask him to imitate what you are doing or just act that you are going to the bathroom, it can be in a potty or toilet. Few encourage their children in this way, letting them live naturally, that is, instead of showing an example to them, they simply leave the children without a diaper and if they soil the rug or the room, the parents go and clean it. But remember, don't exert pressure, sooner or later, the child will drop the nappies.

From time to time, small difficulties may arise, as in most cases, fear. A subject that we will deal with in the next chapter, with the theme of phobias. But now returning to the subject, if, for example; Maria thought that she lost parts of her body seeing the secretions that came out. The mother couldn't understand why Maria desperately screamed when she needed to go to the bathroom, asking for a diaper. But with explanations and reassuring remarks when using the bathroom, the problem was quickly resolved. One thing parents should understand is this: Children who have trouble getting out of nappies never want to annoy or penalize their parents. Maybe they don't quite understand something, they are worried and afraid. At this stage, children need patience, sensitivity, and understanding. Punishments, contempt, and inopportune laughter always cause the concern to worsen or displace, making the solution more and more difficult.

SELF-CONTROL: A FEMALE CHARACTERISTICS?

One of the main differences between boys and girls is that girls learn more easily from their mistakes. According to your experience, do you confirm this? An American psychologist observed one-year-old girls and boys in a doctor's waiting room. While the boys often grabbed objects that their parents had forbidden them to touch. Girls, in general, respected the ban. So just more polite. There is a classic experiment to test the memory and impulse control of eight-month-old babies. In it, an object is hidden somewhere and then, under the eyes of the child, taken to another place, and then, under the eyes of the child, taken to another place. Usually, children look for the object in place, or they cannot resist the urge to look where they have always looked. In one study, male and female babies, over time, we're able to increasingly perform better in the experiment; girls, however, made noticeably greater progress. In general, girls seem to be able to control themselves better than boys. We can see this as well, for example, in tantrums that are normal in children of one and two years and that, at this age, happen with equal frequency in boys and girls. By the third year of life, however, girls have far fewer tantrums and are better able to integrate into day-to-day kindergarten.

How to deal with fear?

All children are afraid, whether they are boys or girls. But don't confuse phobia with fear, both have fear, but phobias are like diseases that may or may not be treated.

We will see this in chapter six with the topic of Reverse Psychology. But before we get to the subject of fears, I quote the scientific facts below.

Scientific Facts

A Harvard psychology professor, in a prospective study, examined the fears of both boys and girls, finding that, even early in life, girls are more fearful than boys. At four months, both sexes reacted in the same way and intensity to unknown stimuli such as; the strong smell, luminous objects in motion, until a different result was obtained with the fourteen-month-old babies. Fearful children had a rapid heartbeat and a greater amount of stress hormones in their blood, their faces were tense and their pupils dilated. They are signals for the activity of the amygdala, an almond-sized nodule in our brain's limbic system, which registers and triggers fear. Because androgens (male hormones) have an effect on these nerve cells, boys show fewer fear reactions. But even in the teacher's opinion, girls' exaggerated fears also have to do with the differentiated care of parents or guardians. Allowing children, whether boys or girls, to go through totally normal experiences, such as falling on the floor or slipping.

While society waits for men to show them their fears, women can do so, and even more so can girls. Therefore, they admit to being afraid more easily than men. It has also been observed that parents often discourage young daughters because they consider certain activities too dangerous or unsuitable for girls. For example, boys are frequently told to defend themselves, while girls learn to accept things and suppress aggression. Anger, being a feeling that everyone knows, also has a function: it helps to defend ourselves and face our challenges, giving us more courage. It is not healthy to suppress anger. Suppressed anger, sooner or later, will become fear! Because our bad feelings, which we are not allowed to, unconsciously come back to us regularly like monsters or bogeymen.

Fear is and cannot be overemphasized, like all other feelings, useful and has its meaning. It represents a warning to be attentive and to check the circumstances carefully. Fear helps us prepare for difficult or unfamiliar situations. Instead of being overcome by fear and being paralysed not knowing what to do, we can take advantage of fear. Fear is energy that can help us solve a problem and overcome a challenge. Let's see fear as a good thing, but not in bad situations representing a bad thing.

We now find ourselves in a new situation, for example, a dentist appointment. It's totally normal to be afraid of something new, but it's not normal for a child or person to have this fear for years, and then we bring up the subject of the phobia (Go to the next chapter).

Whenever we do or experience something new, we are afraid. That's why you should try it: only then can you overcome your fear. Explain to her that fear helps prepare for a situation. But remember that the opposite of fear is hope, and it is hoped that helps us overcome the fear of losing something or someone. The more a child has this positive experience, the better he will deal with fear. Remind your kids that at first they didn't want to ride a bike, but then they learned; that they were afraid of water, but now they bathe in a pool, that they didn't want to go to kindergarten, but now they have learned to socialize better. Another thing that helps in dealing with fear is a physical skill. By discovering the strengths of our bodies, we also learn to master them. It can start with simple games that, above all, men do with their children, making them fly and continue with others such as; fighting and playing horseback. In gymnastics courses for parents and children, it is possible to learn simple and enjoyable exercises. That way, you get to know your child's reactions. Don't make comparisons, follow the children's joy and continue to encourage them about physical activities that, for them, are challenges.

Singing is also the best medicine against fear. You've heard of the expression "Who sings his evils amaze", a good example of a film that shows this is "Girl versus Monsters" produced by Disney. The more she sings, the more she drives away the monsters, and there, the monsters represent fears. If you sing a lot with your children, they will help you create a repertoire of songs that you will find useful in many situations. Songs against fear are also found on cassettes and CDs for children. Don't leave your child singing alone, sing together. With each successful experience, your child's confidence grows and fear decreases. You must have heard that those who sing their evils amaze.

Another proven method for dealing with fears is relaxation exercises. Whoever manages to relax, will face situations that give more self-confidence to fear.

The fears of parents

Parents are often afraid of their children. This is not surprising, because they are aware of the numerous dangers they are exposed to today. It is a necessary fear to some extent because it always reminds parents that they must take seriously their obligations to protect children from harm. Everyone must be wearing a seat belt in the car, hot water and drinks cannot be near a small child without an adult nearby, access to a swimming pool has to be closed off by a fence, and many more things. Even with these careful measures, most accidents with children happen indoors. However, many parents do not know exactly what children are always protected from new experiences to learn to fall to learn to lean on the fall. In our sedentary, automotive society, it has to be repeated over and over again that falling is an important experience for children.

The best way for parents to protect the child is to teach him what can happen in everyday life. Therefore, show the child how to open and close a door, where there is a danger of catching fingers. Demonstrate when a teapot is hot and a lighted match can burn, that one side of the knife is sharp, but we use the unsharpened side, that it is better to get off the sofa with your legs first than with your head. Parents protect the child if they allow him to climb trees, slide down a ravine, balance on fallen tree trunks, play in the mud, and walk backward. Children who learn by experimenting in protected environments are the best protection against accidents.

Surely you have already noticed that there are cautious children and mischievous children, whether they are boys or girls. Cautious children should be encouraged and encouraged to live new experiences. The sleepers should, on the contrary, be able to carry out the necessary experiments within a safe and secure environment. No one can just be free of fears. From time to time, these fears are also seen in public. Imagine that a girl disappeared, was abused, raped, and then murdered, eight months later she is found among a pile of objects or in an abandoned house. We are saddened by the harm that men sometimes do to women and fathers to their daughter's inappropriate actions.

If you don't have your own experiences of violence, your fears are based on cases reported in newspapers, books or on news and television, radio programs. A murder of a girl is always far more prominent news than the fact that every day, many girls lose their lives in car accidents or die of cancer. This means that the media transmit reality in a distorted way. So be aware that your fear was eventually produced by the media. Maybe it's good to remember that you drive a car every day, even though you know that the danger of being fatally injured is greater than being the victim of a violent crime. Or even on the bus, even now with turnstiles and collectors, buses continue to be robbed in some places, so fear can arise from there too.

A German author has written about it, saying that the ongoing concern for people who abuse children, on the one hand, psychologically burdens children and ignores the perpetrators of abuse and rape. In most cases, they are among relatives and close friends. Fears and preventive measures are directed the wrong way at this very moment. Those who understand the subject emphasize that the best protection of children from abuse is self-confidence. Therefore, it is necessary to strengthen self-confidence instead of spreading the less that makes us small.

There is always the possibility of losing the children. That should be a reason to enjoy every day we spend with them more. There is no better protection than confidence and optimism. And every time we laugh together with the child is an important moment. If you knew that a child was going to die, in your child's case, for example. What would you do differently?

There is a very simple rule of family therapy that always holds true: intergenerational boundaries are always respected. You, as an adult, have an obligation and a responsibility to set limits. You as a parent can be as affectionate with your child as he wants. Anything you both like is allowed. If you happen to experience sexual arousal, then the parent's obligation is to stop playing immediately. Child sexuality and adult sexuality cannot be mixed, because children do not know what is good for them. They are submissive to their parents and dependent on them. The adult always has the responsibility for the child and is always the strongest.

Reverse Psychology

WHAT IS REVERSE PSYCHOLOGY?

Reverse psychology is a type of conversation used to convince people to do or think differently from what they are thinking. For example, let's pretend that your friend has just broken up, with that comes those questions in his/her head: What did I do? The problem is mine and not theirs. I don't know what to do, I think it was his/her fault too. And a lot of other tricky and different questions can be found in both teenagers and adults who are dating or being lovers. And so, the first thing you should do in such a situation is to use the famous reverse psychology, and then you ask me: How do I use reverse psychology? And the answer is very simple, try to convince the person with positive words, examples of motivation, solutions, for you who want to become a psychologist it is good to train this type of psychology in people who are having serious issues or similar ones like this example we mentioned before. When a person is in crisis, the best way to calm them down is to use reverse psychology. When the situation involves children, the best way to convince them is by performing fun games or therapies, trying to be friends with this child even if he is one of those messy or overly complicated children. The important thing is to make a friendship between you and the child, as soon as the bonds of friendship increase, your mind will be able to interpret the child's feelings, you will be able to study the child to see what kind of problem he is witnessing.

ID, EGO AND SUPEREGO

The id, ego, and superego are names invented by Freud, he suggested the division of mental life into two different parts: the conscious and the unconscious. The conscious portion, like the visible part of the iceberg, would be small and insignificant, preserving only a superficial view of the entire personality. The unconscious portion, as well as the submerged part of the iceberg, would contain the instincts, that is, the driving forces of all human behaviour. To better understand what the ID, the ego, and the superego are all about, I will explain how they work, and then I will summarize the three words in just a few words that are the basis of everything.

ID

The ID constitutes the reservoir of psychic energy, it is where the life and death drives are located. The characteristics are attributed to the unconscious system. It is governed by the pleasure principle (Psyche that aims only at the pleasure of the individual).

EGO

The ego is the system that establishes the balance between the demands of the id, the demands of reality, and the orders of the superego. The true personality decides whether to accept the decisions of the ID or the Superego.

SUPEREGO

The superego originates with the Oedipus complex, from the internalization of prohibitions, limits, and authority. It's something beyond the ego that is always censoring you and saying: This is not right, don't do it, that is, the one that hurts when we harm someone, is our break. In short, the id is our unconscious side, where it thinks that everything is possible, that everything can be done, that nothing is wrong. The ego is formed from the ID, so it can either follow the ID or obey the superego. The superego is our remote control, that is, it controls us not to do something, it teaches us to maintain control. But not everything can go as planned, in terms of the ego is you, the id is the confused and ambitious part, the superego is the conscious and controlling part.

PHOBIAS

Phobias are not something genetic, some say yes, but the main phobias we acquire throughout life when we go through experiences that cause us some dread, constant fear that even when we quote the word of what we are afraid of, we already feel a chill down our spine, and we were frozen in fear. This is called phobia. See below for some types of phobia, I won't go into too much detail, just say the basics.

ABLUTOPHOBIA

It's the kind of fear of Smudge from Monica's gang, we all know that Smudge is afraid of water, right? Yeah, but here it's different, in this case, the phobia presents the fear of taking a shower.

ACROPHOBIA

Fear of heights, many people are afraid of heights, but some people are afraid of falling, one thing is very different from the other. Fear of heights is related to the fear of any kind of height, but the fear of falling from a high place is already something normal and cannot be considered a type of phobia. Unless the person is afraid of both, then we can say that he has a phobia of heights, acrophobia.

AEROPHOBIA or AVIOPHOBIA

It is the fear related to air travel, many people are afraid of travelling by plane, and I admit that I was also afraid of travelling by plane, so in the case, it may be that if the person faces the fear and seeks the courage to take off and leave for another city outside the country, the best way is to live the experience with time to lose fear and avoid watching movies that involve plane crashes. Of course, plane accidents can happen, but if the pilot is good and the plane is in the right conditions, I guarantee that no accident will happen. You who are afraid of travelling by plane try to forget that you are inside it, close your eyes and make astral travel. We'll talk about astral travel further down. Remember: that in the case of the word Aerophobia, the fear of air travel can also be related to the fear of travelling in other types of transport that are in the air, for example, helicopters, spaceships, but aviophobia is already the fear of travelling by planes, then it cannot be considered a phobia of all air travel. Remember this, it's very important.

AGORAPHOBIA

It is the fear of open, public and crowded places. It is clear then that in this case it is better for the person to carry out a treatment close to home.

AILUROPHOBIA

fear of cats

AMATHOPHOBIA

Fear of dust, dirt, or anything that makes a person weird enough for us to realize how afraid they are of dirt.

ANDROPHOBIA

Fear of men, I believe that we women are already afraid of men when they are aggressive and usually people with this type of phobia may have suffered a lot in childhood and had a trauma that left them with this type of phobia, so they will not want to live with it around men because you won't feel safe.

ANTHROPOPHOBIA

Fear of society is the fear of leaving home and seeing the world because you are afraid of the people who live there.

APHOBIA OR PHOBOPHOBIA

What kind of person has to be afraid of not having a phobia, I think they should feel good about not having phobias, right? Well, I think so too, but no one in the world is born without fear, we are all afraid of something, but aphobia is a totally out-of-the-ordinary feeling.

ARACHNOPHOBIA

Remember the character Ronald Weasley from Harry Potter? That is right. Fear of spiders. For those who have the courage to catch a spider or kill one that is pissing you off, that's fine, but there are those who scream as soon as they see a spider, compared to the cockroach too.

ARITHMOPHOBIA

Who has trouble doing maths homework? Have you figured out what this phobia is? If you thought that it is a phobia of studying mathematics, you are very wrong, this phobia presents people who are afraid of numbers, exactly, numbers! It is strange every phobia that we have already discussed here in this book, but to understand better, let's take a good look at the word.

ARITHMETIC + PHOBIA = ARITMOPHOBIA

ASTRAPHOBIA, BRONTOPHOBIA
OR KERAUNOPHOBIA

Fear of lightning and thunder. Think lightning is camera flashes that take pictures of you, lightning, depending on where you are amazing phenomena and great for temporarily recording and creating home cinema special effects. Thunder is just noise, and who doesn't like to tell horror stories?

ATYCHIPHOBIA

Fear of failing or failing at something.

AUTOMYSOPHOBIA

This type of phobia is different from Amathophobia. Amathophobia is a fear of dirt, but here the person is afraid of getting dirty. Many girls mostly hate getting dirty, a mild phobia that later becomes more active and stronger.

AUTOPHOBIA

Fear of being alone or alone, with no one to keep company.

BALLISTOPHOBIA

It is the fear of bullets and missiles that are fired by guns. The person with this type of phobia cannot see anything resembling a bullet or missile, nor is he able to concentrate if he hears a gunshot.

BASOPHOBIA

A person is afraid of falling or of standing up, and many people who are afraid of heights may actually be afraid of falling or of standing in a high place, but that doesn't mean they are afraid of heights. Good, but in this case, we are talking about people afraid of falling and standing up.

BIOPHOBIA

Everyone who has studied science or biology in life knows that bio means life. All right, if bio means life and phobia equals fear, better known as a mental disorder and exaggerated fear, what does biophobia mean? Biophobia is that person who is afraid of life itself, is afraid of life!

BOTANOPHOBIA

It is a fear of plants. All of them.

HAPHEPHOBIA

I'll give you a hint. Have you heard about the people who are considered as untouchables in India? Have you figured out what the word haphephobia means? Exactly, haphephobia is the fear of being touched by something, not only by people, but also by plants, animals, microorganisms, objects, anything that strikes a person will panic. Strange, isn't it? But the truth is serious, there are people who don't like to be touched, and probably if they don't treat themselves, they will soon live a more complicated life than normal.

CATAPEDAPHOBIA

Now, we can say that this is the kind of fear that almost everyone has, the fear of jumping from high or low places.

CATHISOPHOBIA

People who are afraid to sit down, even if the place is clean and comfortable.

CHOROPHOBIA

What do you like to do besides singing? Listen to music? And what else? To dance? So let's discuss the matter soon, you notice in the name of the type of phobia that it is written Chorophobia, right? Everyone knows that choir is equal to singing a musical choir, but in this case, it is not the fear of singing, but the fear of dancing.

CHRISTIANOPHOBIA

Fear of Christians. It is usually pagans and other religions that have been persecuted by Christians in the past or are still threatened by their differences that make people have this type of phobia.

CHROMOPHOBIA OR CHROMATOPHOBIA

Fear of colours. In this way, a person will never be able to live in an environment, because everywhere the eye perceives colour through light. But just by the name doesn't mean that the person will be afraid of all colours, at most five or seven colours and for each one it can be different. For example, I don't really like black or red because they are colours that bring me depression and anger, but for others it can mean a happy moment and a passion for colour. Just looking at the colours that I don't like, I already feel as if that brings me a negative energy and that ends up bothering me a lot with the feeling of wanting to get away from it.

CHRONOMENTROPHOBIA

Scared of clocks. Unlike the type of phobia mentioned above, here is the fear of being near clocks or hearing a clock.

CHRONOPHOBIA

Afraid of time, not only the time of hours, but the time of life, weather time, the weather in general.

CLAUSTROPHOBIA

I'm sure you know very well, as this is the kind of phobia that people talk about most in films and books. Fear of closed places.

ANTONYM: agoraphobia; fear of open spaces. Such as public spaces, squares, and others.

CLEITHROPHOBIA

Fear of being locked in closed places. Different from the phobia of being in tight or very spacious places. It's easy to confuse claustrophobia with cleithrophobia, but the difference is precisely being locked in closed places in general, it can be small or large. Now claustrophobia is fear of tight spaces, whether the door and window are open or not. Keep an eye out for it.

CLIMACOPHOBIA

Fear of going up or down (falling) the stairs.

CNIDOPHOBIA

The fear of stings or of getting stung by it. Cnidophobia is most commonly triggered due to getting stung by a bee, wasp, stinging plant nettles, or even needles used in medical procedures.

COIMETROPHOBIA

Fear of cemeteries. It's okay that we can't disturb the dead in a cemetery at night, that's like violating the laws of society. But a person with a fear of cemeteries doesn't exactly need to enter a graveyard, they can imagine, watch or see a graveyard that they are already terrified of. If you are afraid of entering cemeteries because of the supernatural, but you are not afraid of seeing an image or hearing the word cemetery, then this is not a phobia.

COMETOPHOBIA

Fear of comets.

COPROPHOBIA

Fear of faeces. It doesn't have to be exactly that of humans, this also goes for the faeces of an animal or insect.

COULROPHOBIA

Scared of clowns. Probably the fear of clowns is due to the joker, Harlech, horror movies with clowns, or the exaggerated laughs they give that look as they will threaten you. I just wonder how clown doctors react to seeing a child or adult scared of them.

CREMNOPHOBIA

Fear of precipices.

CRYOPHOBIA

Fear of intense cold, ice or freezing. In that case, it is better for her not to travel or live in places where it snows and is cold.

CYMOPHOBIA

Fear related to waves, it could be something that is in the shape of waves, it could be the movement of waves, and then the phobia starts. Do not confuse Cymophobia with Cynophobia, they are very different from each other, to understand better see the next type of phobia.

CYNOPHOBIA

The fear of dogs. Usually, this type of phobia is a trauma that was recorded in the person's mind when he watched a film where a dog appeared running or barking angrily at someone, or because he was bitten by a dog the first time he tried to play with one, or maybe it was chased by one and tried to defend himself but got hurt and too many options can lead to that outcome, cynophobia.

DEMONOPHOBIA

Fear of demons. I'm not afraid of demons, but I know they're no good. Don't summon demons and don't ask them for help, they may even be fallen angels, but they are bad influences.

DENDROPHOBIA

Fear of trees. That way the person will never be able to leave the house, there is a law in which it is mandatory to have vegetation, plants, or trees in cities, flats and houses. How will that person breathe, right?

DERMATOSIOPHOBIA, DERMATOPHOBIA or DERMATOPATOPHOBIA

Fear of getting skin diseases. It's okay that we always get sick, but not all skin diseases are contagious or happen all the time. Chickenpox is only once we get it, usually as a child, then we don't get it anymore.

DIPSOPHOBIA

Afraid to drink alcoholic beverages.

DISHABILIOPHOBIA

Fear of getting dressed in front of someone. It doesn't have to be exactly getting dressed in front of a huge audience, it can be just one person there, and the feeling of panic comes over you when you're getting dressed in front of them.

DORAPHOBIA

fear of fur

DROMOPHOBIA

Fear of crossing streets.

DYSTYCHIPHOBIA

Fear of accidents. Nowadays, who is not afraid of being hit by a car or of something horrible happening to you, causing an accident? Accidents are very common in the city where I live, and I assure you that I just don't drive because I'm afraid of accidents and mainly because of neurological and physical health issues that I have, and I can't ignore, but even as a pedestrian and taking public transport, I'm afraid of some time an accident happens.

ELECTROPHOBIA

Fear of electricity.

ENOSIOPHOBIA or ENISSOPHOBIA

Fear of having committed unpardonable sin or criticism. Have you ever wondered in fear even if you've done something horrible before when they ask you about it?

EPISTEMOPHOBIA

Fear of knowledge. How will he/she know the world if he/she is afraid to know himself and others? Explain to me.

ERGASIOPHOBIA

Fear of working or operating (surgeon).

ERGOPHOBIA

Fear of work.

EUROTOPHOBIA

Fear of genitals. So the person will never know itself.

GENOPHOBIA

Fear of sexual abuse. These days, this fear runs deeper, particularly with victims who have had this experience of being abused in private and hidden from the authorities.

HARPAXOPHOBIA

Fear of being robbed. This fear everyone has for sure, who is never afraid of being robbed or mugged in the middle of the street, whether in the morning or at night? I'm always on the lookout.

KATSARIDAPHOBIA

I will admit that I am not afraid of cockroaches, but I am disgusted with them. Many people confuse disgust with fear, and at the time they end up saying that they are afraid of such a thing, when in fact they are disgusted to take it. But there are others who speak the truth, fear cockroaches, a lot of people have it, right?

KINETOPHOBIA OR KINESOPHOBIA

Fear of movements. It's weird, since we move all the time, but it's there.

KOSMIKOPHOBIA

Fear of cosmic phenomena

OIKOPHOBIA

Fear of houses or fear of being in houses. The best way is to camp and stay away from the city.

PHAGOPHOBIA

Fear of swallowing or eating.

SCIOPHOBIA or SCIAPHOBIA

Fear of shadows.

A tip: Find the light within you in the midst of all the darkness.

SCOLECIPHOBIA

Fear of worms and germs. The same goes for those who are afraid of getting dirty or catching skin diseases.

SCOPOPHOBIA or SCOPTOPHOBIA

Fear of being watched or spied on is similar to the fear of changing in front of someone.

SCOTOPHOBIA

Fear of the dark, but not the shadows. Common in children.

SOMNIPHOBIA

Afraid to go to bed. In that case, the only way for the person to sleep would be on the floor. So try to gradually encourage yourself to lie in bed, first start with a thin rug on the floor, then place a soft mattress and gradually increase in size as far as you can and who knows, the phobia of going to bed will pass.

SPECTROPHOBIA

Have you ever heard of the Bloody Mary legend? Scary, isn't it? Well to sum up this kind of fear is the fear of mirrors, it's not exactly your reflection, but the mirror, have you ever thought if you were in another parallel dimension on the other side of the mirror, where you'll soon be after you turn into a ghost or something of the type? That's right. This fear of mirrors may be bizarre, but it's true.

STAUROPHOBIA

Fear of cross or crucifixes. Sounds like vampires, but not, humans are also afraid of crosses. Crosses can represent evil to them.

TACHOPHOBIA

Fear of speed. You will never race on a formula 1 track.

TECHNOPHOBIA

Fear of technology. It is difficult to live without technology now that we are in a time of technological revolution and practically everywhere has technology. Different for people from the countryside, but if you think you can live in nature without relying on technology to communicate with people or prefer to be alone without technology, then that's fine.

TERATOPHOBIA

Fear of children or deformed people. In today's world, I find it difficult for a person to leave the house, mainly because there are many disabled, deformed, and children scattered around.

THALASSOPHOBIA

Fear of the sea. Recommended not to live near the sea.

TOMOPHOBIA

Fear of surgery. And if you need to make one? Can you?

TOPOPHOBIA

Fear of certain places or situations that cause fear and dread

XENOPHOBIA

Fear of foreigners or strange people.

I presented above 98 examples of existing phobias, but there is more than that. The examples I cited are the most feared, but that doesn't mean there aren't others. It is common to be afraid of insects, dark, but now closed places, open places, fear of people and the public, it is something that must be dealt with and quickly. Time to know yourself. Write below twenty types of phobias that you have (you can take the examples given above as well):

____

____

Okay, now that you've mentioned the phobias you have, let's go back to the top and reread the phobias you mentioned again. Then tell me why you have these phobias. The purpose of the test is to make you face your own fears, it's the only way to treat yourself. Think fear is your friend, have courage and face it. It may be difficult at first, but keep going until you get used to it and if you still can't, stop for a while, reflect, and then try again. Ask for help to gain confidence and courage to face your fears too, because that will be very good.

* 9 7 8 9 3 5 6 1 0 2 2 0 0 *